This special edition of

A BOOKMARK

Texas A&M University Press

is limited to

750 copies.

A Bookmark

NUMBER TEN:

The Joe and Betty Moore Texas Art Series

A Bookmark

TEXAS A&M UNIVERSITY PRESS

Henry C. Dethloff

TEXAS A&M UNIVERSITY PRESS
College Station

First edition

*Publication of this volume
is made possible
by a generous grant
from Joe and Betty Moore.*

The paper used in this book
meets the minimum requirements
of the American National Standard for Permanence
of Paper for Printed Library Materials, z39.48-1984.
Binding materials have been chosen for durability.
∞

Library of Congress Cataloging-in-Publication Data

Dethloff, Henry C.
A bookmark : Texas A&M University Press / Henry C. Dethloff. —
1st ed.
p. cm.—(Joe and Betty Moore Texas art series ; no. 10)
Includes bibliographical references (p.) and index.
ISBN 0-89096-878-0 (acid-free paper)
1. Texas A&M University Press—History. 2. University
presses—United States—History—20th century. 3. University
presses—Texas—History—20th century. I. Title. II. Series.
Z473.T44D48 1999
070.5'94—dc21 99-17968
CIP

FOR

Frank H. Wardlaw,
Jack K. Williams, John H. Lindsey, and
Joe and Betty Moore

Contents

List of Illustrations, XI

CHAPTERS

1. The Beginning, 3
2. Air, Earth, Fire, and Water, 35
3. Up from the Ashes, 63
4. Making Books, 91
5. Strategic Planning, 121

Notes, 141

Index, 153

Illustrations

1. Frank Wardlaw, 7
2. Jack Kenney Williams, 11
3. E. M. "Buck" Schiwetz, John H. Lindsey, and Frank Wardlaw, 12
4. The Old Board of Directors Building, 14
5. Pressmark, 16
6. *Between Sun and Sod,* 19
7. Joe and Betty Moore stand with Frank Wardlaw, 23
8. *Storms Brewed in Other Men's Worlds,* 27
9. *Grasses of Texas,* 29
10. *Black Jack,* 31
11. The Advisory Council of Texas A&M University Press, 38
12. *The Stolen Steers,* 44
13. *Junks of Central China,* 46
14. *Early Texas Oil,* 48
15. Lloyd Lyman, 50
16. Board of Directors Building burned on February 28, 1979, 58
17. Texas A&M University Centennial commemorative pewter plate, 59
18. Burned letter written by Tom Lea to Frank Wardlaw, 60
19. John H. Lindsey, 65
20. Frank E. Vandiver, 67
21. Frank W. R. Hubert, 68
22. *Yassı Ada,* 76
23. Jack K. Williams and Frank Wardlaw chat with E. M. "Buck" Schiwetz, 85
24. Press staff, 1984, 86
25. *Black Art in Houston,* 87
26. Finis F. Collins and Ivan McDougal, 88

27. Lady Bird Johnson, 92
28. *Lost in West Texas*, 98
29. *East of Chosin*, 103
30. *Equal before the Lens*, 105
31. *Lure of the Land*, 110
32. *In the Sporting Tradition*, 117
33. *The Fightin' Texas Aggie Band*, 119
34. *Shadows of Vietnam*, 133
35. *George Herbert Walker Bush*, 134
36. *Land of the Desert Sun*, 135
37. *Heralds of Spring in Texas*, 136

COLOR PLATES
following page 34

Texas Heartland
Old Ranches of the Texas Plains
Buck Schiwetz' Aggieland
Fishes of the Gulf of Mexico
Texas Wildlife
The Natural World of the Texas Big Thicket
The Texas Gulf Coast
Kelly Blue
Landscapes of Texas
The Texas Hill Country
Coastal Texas
Pecos to Rio Grande
The Deer Pasture
The John H. Lindsey Building
Texas in Bloom
Frank Reaugh
A Flying Tiger's Diary
Plantation Life in Texas
The Mapping of the American Southwest
The Nature of Texas
Cowboy Spurs and Their Makers

The Art of Tom Lea
Lighthouses of Texas
Plains Farmer
O'Neil Ford
Quest for the Presidency 1992
Lone Star Dinosaurs
Texas Art and a Wildcatter's Dream
Planetary Astronomy
Journeys into Czech Moravian Texas
Trogons, Laughing Falcons, and Other Neotropical Birds

TABLE 1
Texas A&M University Press, Net Sales by Fiscal Years, 1975–76 to 1983–84, 83

A Bookmark

Chapter 1

THE BEGINNING

On September 3, 1974, Frank Wardlaw sent Texas A&M University President Jack K. Williams, a historian, a lengthy memorandum announcing the beginning of the Texas A&M University Press (TAMUP). Wardlaw had begun drafting the memorandum on September 1, the day the press officially came into being. Seizing what he believed to be a special moment in history, Wardlaw sat down to record the "considerable thought that I have devoted to this enterprise since agreeing to undertake it." This letter, he explained, would "serve as an informal memorandum on the new Texas A&M University Press—its establishment, its objectives, its program, its financial structure, and its relationship to the University."[1]

With that memorandum, the history of the new press began—a history that Wardlaw perceived to be closely intertwined with the histories of its parent university, the students and former students who called themselves Texas Aggies, and the university's faculty and administration, as well as with his own past. With great deliberation and forethought, the press's first director created a future for a new publishing enterprise located on the campus of Texas' first public institution of higher learning—the former Agricultural and Mechanical College of Texas, known for the past decade as Texas A&M University (TAMU). In this document, he described the motivations and aspirations behind the creation of this fledgling literary endeavor.

A hundred years earlier, critics had argued that locating an agricultural and mechanical college near Bryan, Texas, was "a sure guarantee that no good will ever be derived from it" and that the lands there were among the poorest in the state, unfit and unhealthy. Similarly, in 1974, many doubted the efficacy of establishing a new university press at what many still considered the Agricultural and Mechanical College of Texas, a "cow college" where the "soil" was hardly suitable for cultivating literary endeavors of any value.[2] Besides, Texas universities already had a press, and a good one at that, established at the University of Texas in Austin by this very same Frank Wardlaw. Anyway, local pundits wryly observed, Texas A&M already had its own printing press where the reports, pamphlets, and catalogs of the university were printed. It hardly made sense for a state or a college to have two presses.

Times were not propitious. Even Wardlaw was explicit about that: "Many of the nation's scholarly presses are experiencing financial difficulties, difficulties engendered by the near bankruptcy of so many colleges and universities, the tightening of the market for academic books, and the rapidly rising cost of all elements which go into the production and distribution of books. On the face of it, it would seem that a new press, with no income from a large backlist to support it, would have limited chance of success."[3]

"We are undergoing a revolution in scholarly publishing in this country," Wardlaw wrote in 1975 to W. H. Patterson, president of the University of South Carolina. Following the 1973 embargo placed on exports of oil from the nation members of the Organization of Petroleum Export Countries (OPEC), inflation had become rampant, reaching into double digits. Banks, businesses, universities, and scholarly presses alike were struggling against spiraling costs and even insolvency. Many university presses had eliminated royalties on their scholarly books. Others were entering the commercial book market with popularly marketed "trade" publications and textbooks. Some simply had ceased to exist.[4] Why, then, another university press? And why now?

"What can a Press do for A&M?" Wardlaw sought to address the unease, confusion, and even ignorance that existed concerning the concept and proposed development of a university press. A press, Wardlaw believed, would "stimulate scholarly productivity of the broadest type on the campus." Many of the faculty published under other university or private press imprints. Many published their work principally in journals and extension bulletins. Wardlaw thought that many of the latter were "capable of producing books of lasting importance," and an A&M Press would encourage this type of scholarly endeavor. While articles and bulletins are indispensable and important, he added, they tend to be ephemeral, while *books endure.*[5]

"By making the products of A&M's scholarly research more broadly available . . . the Press can further one of the principal objectives of the University, *which is constantly to expand the horizons of useful knowledge.*" Wardlaw strongly believed that, "through a responsible program of regional publication, the Press can preserve and interpret Texas' peculiar heritage in books of regional history, art, literature, and folklore. . . . A Press can help Texans understand the beauty and mysteries of their own segment of the natural world." It can help Texans appreciate the achievements of their artists and writers and help them solve the many problems that must be solved. It is the "inescapable obligation" of a university press, Wardlaw asserted, to serve the people of the state to which it belonged.[6]

A press, he advised TAMU President Jack Williams, can "provide an effective medium for extending the educational thrust of the University." It can enhance the national and international value and reputation of its programs. It can play a significant role in helping the university strengthen its programs in the humanities and social sciences, and it can be an important instrument for enhancing the prestige of the university. While Wardlaw stressed the role of the new press as a regional one, he emphasized that the press must never publish "inferior books simply because they are about Texas." If there was a basic value Wardlaw ascribed to his mission and that of TAMUP, that value was integrity. "Integrity," he wrote in a letter to Henry Winkler, then chairing the board of the Rutgers University Press, "is an old-fashioned word," but "that's what university presses are basically all about."[7]

Wardlaw knew what university presses were all about. Texas A&M's was the third university press he had established. He came to Texas A&M through a long, circuitous route beginning with his birth in South Carolina on August 16, 1913. Having grown up a preacher's son, he worked one year in a cotton mill after finishing high school and decided that there were better ways to make a living. Then Wardlaw enrolled at the University of South Carolina to study journalism. At age twenty-one, he contracted tuberculosis, lost the use of one lung, and spent almost a full year "flat on his back." That year, largely spent reading and listening to opera, shaped much of Wardlaw's subsequent career, as well as his attitude toward—and appreciation of—life.

In his third semester at the university, Frank's father died, and he was forced to drop out of school and find work. At the height of the Great Depression, the only work readily available to young men was with the Civilian Conservation Corps (CCC), a New Deal agency that offered work mostly in reforestation and conservation projects. The pay was $16.00 per month plus room and board, with half that salary going to the laborers' parents. Wardlaw became editor of the CCC camp newspaper. That job soon led to employment with the *Columbia (S.C.) Record* as a proofreader, at a salary of $12.50 per week. Six weeks later, Frank was promoted to reporter, making $15.00 per week.[8]

When World War II came along, Wardlaw's medical history (tuberculosis, malaria, and a failed lung) made him unfit for military service. Recently married as well as physically ineligible for the draft, he was hired by the University of South Carolina to teach journalism, head up the university's news and information bureau, and serve as sports information director. The university's faculty rapidly was being depleted as the men entered military service. When the war ended, the new president of the university, Admiral Norman Smith, had a book he wanted published. In 1945, Smith gave Wardlaw the job of publishing it, simultaneously appointing him "director" of the previously nonexistent University of South Carolina Press. Wardlaw recalled that publishing experience as a very satisfying one.[9] It marked the beginning of the University of South Carolina Press and of his long career in university publishing.

In 1949, the University of Texas, interested in starting its own press, invited Wardlaw to interview for the job of director. Wardlaw never had been to Texas and wanted to see it, so he came—and remained. He advised the administrators and distinguished faculty that he lacked what might be considered an essential ingredient for an academic post, particularly that of director of a university press. He offered to remedy that by pursuing an undergraduate degree at the University of Texas on the side. Walter Prescott Webb, already famous as a historian of Texas and the West, advised him that having no degree at all would be a lot more distinguished (and certainly more distinctive) than having a bachelor's degree. If he had a B.A., people would wonder why he did not have a master's degree. If he had an M.A., they would think he should have a doctorate. And a Ph.D., Webb thought, really would not provide any special qualifications for the job! So Wardlaw accepted the post.

FIG. 1. *Frank Wardlaw, founding director of the University of South Carolina Press (1945) and the University of Texas Press (1949), came to Texas A&M University to begin his third university press in 1974.*

Subsequently, Walter Prescott Webb, folklorist J. Frank Dobie, and naturalist Roy Bedicek played major roles in Wardlaw's life and that of the new University of Texas Press (UTP).[10] Within two decades, the press had become one of the nation's leading regional university publishing establishments. Its proud list of books focused on Texas, the Southwest, and Latin America, emphasizing these areas' history and literature.

In addition to heading UTP, Wardlaw became an active member of the prestigious Texas Institute of Letters, serving twice as its president. He also served two terms as president of the Association of American University Presses. He wrote a book, *"I Have That Honor": Tributes to J. Frank Dobie* (1965), as well as many articles in such popular magazines as *Harper's* and the *Saturday Review*. He became a popular speaker and a highly esteemed raconteur.[11]

During these years in Austin, Wardlaw's wife, Jane Williamson, the mother of his four mostly grown children, died. In 1970, he married Rosemary Leonard Boynton, a native of Junction City, Kansas, and the mother of five children (four sons and a daughter). Rosemary, who was head of the Peace Corps's office on the University of Texas campus, met Frank at a party for sociologists from Huston-Tillotson College and the University of Texas. At the time, she thought that her future husband had something to do with newspapers.[12] Following their wedding, Rosemary became a vital part of Frank Wardlaw's life and publishing career.

Why, at the very height of his career at the successful University of Texas Press, did Frank Wardlaw decide to go to Texas A&M University? An interesting tale lies behind what is sometimes referred to as a "career quirk." Wardlaw explained a good part of his reasoning in an article appearing in 1976 in *Scholarly Publishing,* a journal produced at the University of Toronto and geared toward scholarly authors and publishers. He was visiting a new and good friend, John H. Lindsey, at the latter's beach house on Galveston Island in September, 1973: "I stood in the kitchen of the beach house . . . glowering into a glass of iced tea and complaining about something that was happening at the University of Texas, that great and tortured university which has had more than its share of troubles in recent years. 'I am surrounded,' I said, 'by an entirely new Phalanx of Pharaohs who know not Joseph.'"[13]

Wardlaw's problems at the University of Texas were manifold but often subtle. The University of Texas was growing up and trying to shake free of its Texas roots. Some critics found Wardlaw's apparent preoccupation with Texas and regional topics parochial and called the press the "cow chip press." Faculty members thought that the university press should focus more on truly "intellectual" issues and topics. Eastern Europe, sociology, and economics were much in vogue. In November, 1974, only a few months after his arrival in College Station, Wardlaw commented to his good friend Alfred A. Knopf, head of one of America's leading commercial presses: "I, too, am worried about the way things are going at the University of Texas. It is headless and aimless at present." The climate at UT, he said, was "generally disgruntled."[14]

At the time, Rosemary Wardlaw recalled, she and Frank had no inclination to seek employment or a home elsewhere. The University of Texas Press had been the center of Wardlaw's life; at sixty-two years of age, he was beginning to think about retirement, not another career in publishing.[15]

Into this milieu stepped Texas A&M University, the Texas Aggies (Former Students), and, more specifically, John H. Lindsey, a Houston insurance man and a member of A&M's Class of 1944. After graduation, he had returned to Houston and entered the insurance business with his father. He began to attend the weekly meetings of the Houston chapter of Texas A&M Association of Former Students, held at the Rice Hotel. He recalls that, on one occasion, he entered the meeting late, in the midst of a discussion about "something." The speaker asked if anyone in the group was from Lamar High School. Lindsey held up his hand while taking a seat, not realizing that he was volunteering to help recruit athletes from Lamar for enrollment at A&M. For Lindsey, it was the beginning of dual careers—one in insurance and the other as an Aggie booster. In his life thereafter, Texas A&M affairs often took priority over all other interests.[16]

At his beach house, Lindsey commiserated with his friend about the situation in Austin and, only half in jest, said that he thought the Wardlaws ought to break loose of all that and come to Texas A&M University, "where you will be appreciated and [can] start a new press."[17] Lindsey remembered that both Wardlaws looked at him sharply, almost stunned, but said nothing.

When Wardlaw published his own account of the decision to go to Texas A&M, he recalled the exchange differently (perhaps feeling that he never had been at a loss for words). Intended for a wider audience, these published "recollections" were meant to be instructional rather than literal history. In his account of the exchange with Lindsey, Wardlaw wrote that his response was, "You can't be serious. . . . There has never been a worse time in history to start a new press." Furthermore, he recalled,

> *I didn't really take the conversation seriously. After all I had been in Austin for twenty-four years, our publication program was not in financial trouble, and I was only five years away from compulsory retirement. I knew little about A&M except that it had national stature in such fields as agriculture, engineering, and veterinary medicine, that in every war it had supplied more officers for the Army than any institution except West Point, and finally that it had, within the past ten years, abandoned compulsory military training and begun admitting women to all of its programs. . . . I must confess that I shared the prevailing liberal arts contempt for "cow colleges."*[18]

However the conversation transpired, it jarred Lindsey into action. Although he really never had thought of Texas A&M's having a university press, he realized that it might be a good thing. A few hours after the conversation with Wardlaw, Lindsey decided to call Texas A&M's President Jack Williams and let him know that he had just suggested to Frank Wardlaw that he come to Texas A&M and start a new press.[19] What would the president of Texas A&M think of such a proposal?

Williams had become president of TAMU on November 1, 1970, following the distinguished administration of soldier, statesman, and educator James Earl Rudder. A historian, author, and publicist, Williams[20] liked books and was receptive to the idea, but his top priority role was as an administrator.

"How much would it cost?" Williams asked.

Lindsey replied, "I don't know. We need to look into it and find out."

Finally, after more conversation, Williams said, "John, if you will get three members of the Board of Directors to say okay, I will look into it."

Lindsey then proceeded to telephone three members of TAMU's Board of Directors (now Regents). He called Ford D. Albritton, Jr., of Bryan; William H. Lewie of Waco; and Clyde H. Wells, of Granbury, who was president of the board. Each of them first asked, "How much will it cost?" and then agreed that it should be "looked into." Within three hours of their initial conversation, Lindsey had Williams back on the phone. He reported that three regents agreed that the matter of a press for A&M should be "looked into."[21]

Meanwhile, after a few days, Wardlaw called Lindsey and said, "John, do you remember saying something about me coming to Texas A&M? I am interested in talking about it."[22]

"Frank," Lindsey replied, "we are way ahead of you." He explained to Wardlaw about his conversations with President Williams and the board members. Two weeks later, Williams telephoned Wardlaw, asking him to meet with him in Austin to discuss the possibility of a new university press at TAMU.[23]

In early August, 1973, Williams and Lindsey drove together to Austin for the meeting. Williams never had met Wardlaw but knew of him; in publishing, he was already legendary. Lindsey told him how he had been introduced to Wardlaw by his good friend E. M. "Buck" Schiwetz—a Texas Aggie and an artist famed for his paintings of Texas farm and coastal scenes—at a party given in Austin for Bertha Dobie, J. Frank Dobie's wife. The Dobies were good friends of the Wardlaws. Lindsey had had a wonderful time there and had enjoyed Wardlaw thoroughly. The latter had seized the opportunity

FIG. 2. *Jack Kenney Williams, president of Texas A&M (1970–77) and chancellor of the Texas A&M University System (1977–79). President Williams's dedication to the growth of Texas A&M led him to recognize the importance of a press to the reputation of the university.*

to importune Lindsey to help him convince Schiwetz to produce a series of paintings that the University of Texas Press could publish in book form.[24] Lindsey did so with considerable enthusiasm; as a result, Schiwetz agreed, and the University of Texas published the very elegant *The Schiwetz Legacy: An Artist's Tribute to Texas, 1910–1971.*

In the interim, Lindsey, Schiwetz, and Wardlaw had become fast friends. Their "deer hunting" included hunts and visits at the ranch of Fred Gibson, author of *Old Yeller.* Frank and Rosemary Wardlaw also frequently joined John and Sara Lindsey at Astro baseball games in Houston and sometimes accepted Lindsey's invitation to use the beach house in Galveston.[25] Now Jack Williams was to join the circle.

Wardlaw, Williams, and Lindsey met at the Vagabond Hotel, an un-

FIG. 3. *E. M. "Buck" Schiwetz, John H. Lindsey, and Frank Wardlaw in Wardlaw's offices, 1975. Schiwetz was then Texas A&M University's artist-in-residence, living and working in an apartment in the rear of the Old Board of Directors Building.*

likely place to which Wardlaw directed them, since rumors would fly if he was seen in a public place in Austin with such well-known Texas Aggies.[26] At the meeting, Wardlaw explained to Williams why these were not good times to begin a university press. Costs were at an all-time high, many universities were cutting back or abolishing their presses, and a new press would have no backlist to generate income. Williams responded by observing that Texas A&M was the fastest-growing major university in the country and that it led institutions in the Southwest in the number of National Merit Scholars enrolled. He also said that Texas A&M's administration and Board of Directors were committed to strengthening the liberal arts programs, to building a research library, and to creating a world-class university. A press was a logical step along this path.[27]

In November, 1973, Frank and Rosemary Wardlaw arrived in College Station. Jack Williams asked Haskell Monroe (a professor of history who recently had been appointed dean of faculties) to meet them at the new Holiday Inn and show them around. It was, Monroe recalled, the first he had heard that Texas A&M was interested in establishing a press.[28]

John Lindsey remembers that, during the Wardlaws' visit, he stopped by the old Board of Directors Building to pick up Buck Schiwetz, who was on campus staying in guest quarters there. While he went to get Schiwetz, the Wardlaws got out of the car and began walking around the building and its grounds. When everyone had settled in the car, Wardlaw asked Lindsey what this building was and what it was used for. It was basically empty and unused, he responded, and the administration was thinking about tearing it down. "Don't tear it down!" Wardlaw exclaimed.[29] It would be the perfect setting for the new Texas A&M University Press. At that point, Wardlaw became fully committed to this "new enterprise." The Wardlaws liked what they saw at TAMU:

> *As we walked about the campus the boys said "Howdy" to their elders and the girls said "Hi." We were offered as headquarters for the press a wonderful old post-Victorian building, surrounded by live oaks, which for sixty years had served as headquarters for the board of directors. Suddenly I found myself growing more and more excited at the prospect of building a new press in such an environment during my final years of publishing rather than continuing to fight the same old battles every year. Before we left College Station we were committed to the new adventure.*[30]

In late August, 1974, the Wardlaws arrived on campus and took up residence in the new press director's quarters on the ground floor of the old Board of Directors Building. The press's offices were located on the second floor. Buck Schiwetz soon moved into a suite in the rear of the building as A&M's first "artist-in-residence." Wardlaw intended to see that Schiwetz produced a special set of paintings of Texas A&M scenes.

Rosemary Wardlaw recalls that time as the beginning of "a rare and wonderful lifestyle." Schiwetz, she said, was a high point in that experience.

FIG. 4. *The Old Board of Directors Building, Texas A&M University, drawn by E. M. "Buck" Schiwetz for publication as one of eight prints of campus scenes in the portfolio* Buck Schiwetz' Aggieland, *1975.*

The press's building was more than spacious. It was "marvelous" but dingy. The Wardlaws' ground-floor apartment contained three bedrooms, each with a private bath. She had to "spread out" their rather meager furnishings to give the quarters the appearance of being furnished. Seven additional rooms and private baths were located upstairs; these became the press's offices. Rosemary's life centered around the duties of housekeeper and hostess. She even made drapes. The Wardlaws entertained a lot. Never a week went by without company. After Aggie football games, the Wardlaws' home and the press's offices were a popular gathering place. For all practical purposes, home and office were one and the same.[31]

Late every evening, the Wardlaws would stroll the quiet campus with their two Scotch terriers. Often they encountered an occasional Aggie going to or from the library or the Memorial Student Center, or heading for the dormitories. "Howdy," the passersby inevitably called out. "Howdy," the Wardlaws would respond. It was, Frank Wardlaw commented many times, a happy campus, and for the Wardlaws it was a happy time.[32] Work and play became indistinguishable.

Wardlaw threw himself into his new assignment with exuberance. He asked his friend Tom Lea to design a logo for the new press and its stationery. On September 13, the new stationery was in hand. Frank wrote to Jack Schulman, director of Cambridge University Press, "on our new stationery, which was designed by Tom Lea, to tell you that the Texas A&M Press is now in business." Lea also designed the press's mark, a pictograph representing the basic elements of fire, air, earth, and water. These not coincidentally represented TAMU's interests as both a land-grant and a sea-grant college. "Our offices and living quarters," Wardlaw wrote, "are all that could be desired. . . . We are happy to be embarking on this new adventure." He invited Schulman to visit. "Our apartment, in the same fine old building which houses our offices, has three spare bedrooms and four spare baths."[33]

At that moment, the press staff included its director, Frank Wardlaw; an editor, Margaret Ingram; and an assistant to the director, Gayla Christiansen. It was, as Wardlaw defined it, "a small, highly professional and productive staff." He would add new positions only as needed.[34]

A native Texan and the daughter of an A&M former student, Margaret Ingram was a graduate of Mount Holyoke College with a graduate degree from Cambridge University; she had undertaken further studies at Yale University. After working for Wardlaw at the University of Texas Press in 1969–71, she had left to do freelance editing for that press and for Harvard University Press. She then accepted a position as editor for Resources for the Future, Inc., in Washington, D.C. Wardlaw deemed Ingram "one of the best and most productive editors I have ever had."[35]

Three years earlier, Gayla Eppright Christiansen had relocated to College Station from Kansas City, Missouri, where she held a full-time position in the finance division of American Multi-Cinema, Inc., while also working toward her master's degree.

From the post of administrative assistant to the director of TAMU's Office of Continuing Education and Engineering Extension Service, Christiansen came to TAMUP as assistant to the director and managed the general operations of the press. She was named promotion manager in 1978 and, in 1982, marketing manager. She provided the special insight and administrative experience that enabled the press to begin operating while en-

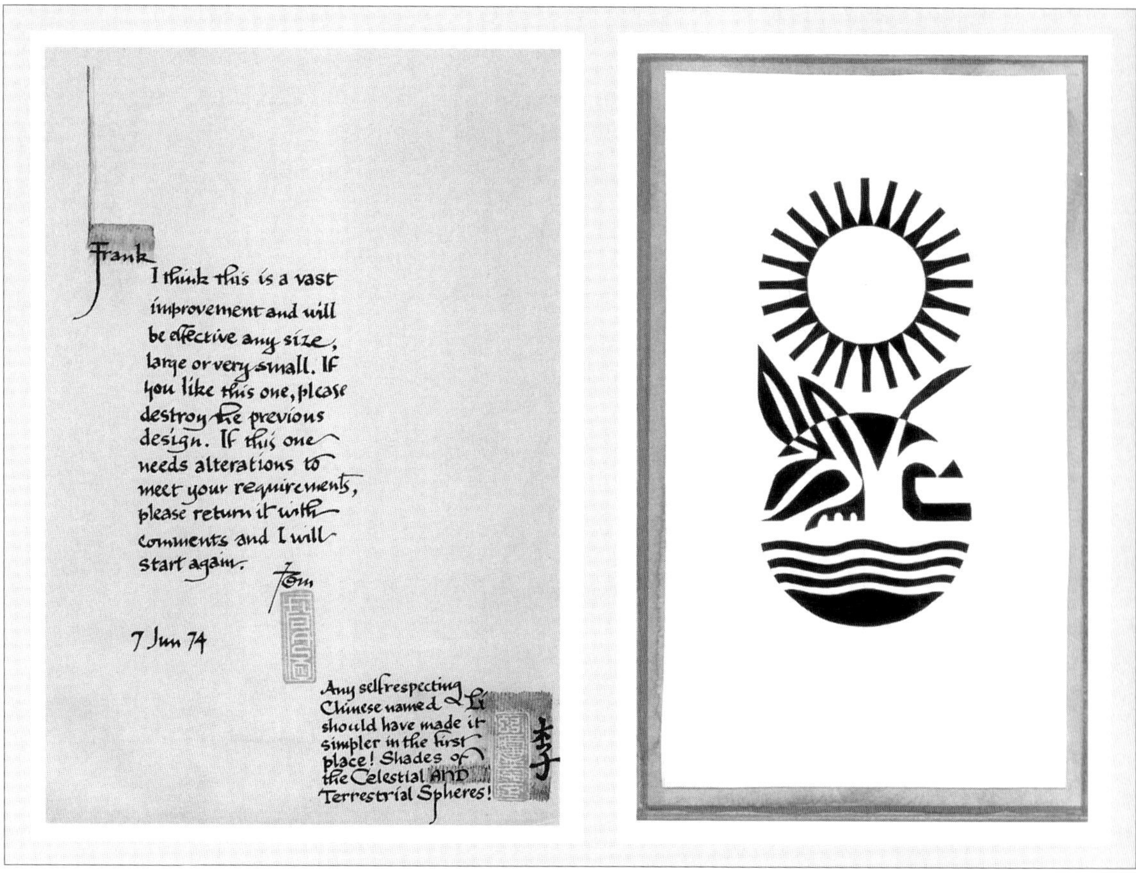

FIG. 5. *El Paso artist Tom Lea went through several drafts of the pressmark before presenting the final drawing to Frank Wardlaw in June 1974. The pressmark represents the basic elements of fire, air, earth, and water and symbolizes the University's concern with all aspects of the environment.*

countering relatively few administrative snags within the context of the increasingly complex TAMU management system.[36]

Another product of the "considerable thought" that Wardlaw had given the new publishing enterprise was Raymond M. Grimaila. One of the nation's leading book designers, Grimaila, in seven out of the past eight years, had placed a book among the top books selected annually by the American Institute of Graphic Arts (AIGA). These books, designated as the nation's best designed, were selected from thousands of titles published each year by university and commercial presses. His art and design work had been featured in a number of solo exhibitions, including a recent AIGA show in New York.[37]

Wardlaw's powers of persuasion and his reputation were such that Grimaila agreed to leave Wesleyan University Press, where he had served with distinction for fourteen years, to come to Texas A&M to work as Wardlaw's design and production manager. On September 14, Grimaila and his wife, Ruth, made their first visit to TAMU, Bryan, and College Station. They stayed in the Wardlaws' quarters at the press building and for several days dined on Texas steak, barbecue, and Aggie hospitality.[38]

The hospitality, which included seats in the president's box at an Aggie football game, was provided in part by the Texas A&M University Association of Former Students, then directed by Richard O. ("Buck") Weirus. For Texas Aggies, a commitment made by the TAMU president, Board of Regents, and their classmates entailed a commitment by all Aggies. Buck Weirus and the Former Students joined in supporting the new publishing venture by providing Wardlaw with special funds for recruiting key staff. The Former Students also conferred upon Wardlaw the administrative rank of "dean," enabling the association to provide an unrestricted personal administrative fund for the press director (as it did for all deans and department heads). Weirus and John Lindsey both commented later that whatever Wardlaw wanted, Wardlaw got.

With such enthusiastic support, from the top of the Aggie infrastructure to its bottom, Wardlaw felt good about the opportunities for the press. So did Ray Grimaila. The Grimailas, Ray and Ruth, scheduled their move from Massachusetts to College Station for February, 1975. Grimaila agreed to help design and produce the initial titles even before the move.[39]

Beyond recruiting and retaining a strong professional staff, the key to success for a university press—especially in the uncertain world of university budgets and finance—was a strong and enduring financial base. Wardlaw was fully cognizant that, financially, these were not good times for university presses. In times of budget constraints and cutbacks, administrators and even faculty sometimes regard a university press as superfluous—nice if you can afford it, but not essential. Besides, a university press generally was not a "line" administrative unit, which meant that, in the political and financial life of a university, its clout was minimal. Too many defunct and financially strapped university presses already littered academia. Wardlaw was determined that TAMUP never should become such a victim. To achieve real independence and integrity for the press would require a substantial degree of financial independence. Thus a considerable part of his "considerable thought" and planning went into financial management.

The key to that financial management was the establishment of restricted revolving funds, each supporting a specific series of books. Those series would be designed to articulate and fulfill the overall mission of the press. That mission, as Wardlaw conceived it, was tripartite: to preserve and interpret Texas' peculiar heritage through books on regional history, art, literature, and folklore; to produce works in the natural and social sciences in all related areas of scholarship that focused on Texas and the Southwest; and to publish books in those programs at Texas A&M University that held national and international value and repute.

The mission was reasonably clear, but how would Wardlaw set the course of the new press so that it not only could, but to an extent *must*, fulfill that mission? He did it by establishing designated revolving funds, each of which independently was committed to the publication of a certain kind of book. Collectively, the types of books and their respective funds would implement the overall mission of the press.

To begin with, Wardlaw received a commitment from President Jack Williams to establish a $200,000 capital revolving fund that would become the press's basic operating fund. On September 18, Wardlaw received confirmation from TAMU's Vice President for Business Affairs Tom D. Cherry that the $200,000 capital revolving fund had been created in Account No. 18909. But Wardlaw detected a problem. Not only did the capital fund need to be established, but also it needed to be allowed to operate free of "Board of Control" regulations. A university account beginning with a numeral "1," he knew, would require that composition, printing, and binding contracts be approved at a "higher" level. On occasion, this might mean that quality could be sacrificed to expediency. Wardlaw wrote to Cherry in protest and sent a copy to Williams. More meetings and letters ensued. Finally, the "oversight" was corrected. Expenditures from the capital revolving fund would be at the director's authorization. Seventy-five percent of the receipts from sales were to be returned to the revolving fund, with 25 percent being used in a general account by the press to cover expenses other than manufacturing.[40]

One of Wardlaw's first targeted book funds grew out of Texas A&M

FIG. 6. *Art also made a perfect match with text in Willie Newbury Lewis's book* Between Sun and Sod, *about her husband's experience ranching in the Texas Panhandle. This H. D. Bugbee illustration for the book, which the press republished in 1976, is typical of the openness and freedom of style of that Panhandle artist. Courtesy Panhandle-Plains Historical Museum*

University's efforts to celebrate its one hundredth birthday. On October 4, 1975, TAMU began celebrating its centennial. Planning for the event had begun on September 23, 1969, when President James Earl Rudder appointed a centennial faculty advisory committee. Rudder asked Homer Lloyd Heaton, dean of admissions, to chair the committee; members included Joseph Milton Nance, head of the history department, and Edward John Romieniec, dean of the College of Architecture. The committee was charged with outlining general plans for the centennial observance. Proposals were to be submitted to the TAMU Board of Directors at its November, 1969, meeting. The proposals that went forward included production of a scholarly history of the university, as well as beautification and enhancement of the campus, for the purpose of making the centennial year "one of the most eventful years in the history of this University."[41] That aspiration and the proposed history had some influence on the decision to establish a Texas A&M University Press.

In October, 1969, Nance approached a newly hired member of the faculty and asked him if he would be interested in writing a history of TAMU.

The faculty member, who was uncertain that he *would* be interested but certain that he *should* be interested, responded pleasantly that he would like to take on the project. Work began in February, 1971. By August, 1972, the 1,027-page first draft of a very comprehensive history had been completed. But what was to be done with the manuscript? Nance, whose several volumes on the Republic of Texas (published by the University of Texas Press) were already considered classics, thought that perhaps the University of Texas Press would consider publishing the A&M history. This idea was not widely disseminated; in light of the tradition of rivalry between UT and TAMU, it was considered heretical. If a history of TAMU were to be published, surely it must be published by a TAMU press.

There, with reviews and revisions of the manuscript in progress, matters rested until Jack K. Williams was installed as the seventeenth president of TAMU. Williams appointed a new committee to review the draft of the centennial history. This committee was chaired by Buck Weirus, director of the Association of Former Students, and included Marion Thomas Harrington, a former A&M president and chancellor; Frank Hubert, dean of education; Clyde Freeman, comptroller; Bob Cherry, secretary of the TAMU Board of Directors; and Henderson Shuffler, historian and director of the Institute of Texan Cultures in San Antonio.[42] By the end of 1973, a final review had been completed.

When Wardlaw arrived, he was presented with a fait accompli—a publishable history of Texas A&M University. It was obvious that the work could not be contained in a single printed volume, so Wardlaw suggested that the centennial history be published in two volumes in a handsome slipcase edition. He and Williams also thought that a briefer pictorial history should be prepared from the text of the larger study. The problem now was how to fund these rather formidable publications. Weirus, Lindsey, and the Association of Former Students provided the answer. Wardlaw estimated the costs of publication to be in the neighborhood of $75,000. The Former Students offered to provide the entire $75,000, with the understanding that receipts from sale of the books would be reinvested in the Centennial Series of the Association of Former Students. This offer gave the press two titles waiting for publication, *A Centennial History of Texas A&M University, 1876–1976* and *A Pictorial History of Texas A&M University, 1876–1976,* as well as a revolving fund. Wardlaw also used funding for the Centennial Series to publish *Buck Schiwetz' Aggieland: A Portfolio of Eight Scenes from Texas A&M University* and a series of postcards derived from Jim Bones's color photographs illustrating *A Pictorial History.*

Wardlaw had a keen interest in creating and publishing a Texas art series, a natural history guide series, and an oil history series. By early October, 1974, his search for prospective authors and artists resulted in a number of formidable artist/photographer/author candidates for the art series, a book in progress for the natural history series, and a candidate to write a pictorial history of the Texas petroleum industry. With gasoline prices having soared over the past few years from an average of twenty-five cents a gallon to one dollar and twenty-five cents a gallon, petroleum was uppermost in the minds of Texans and most American consumers in 1974. A petroleum history series seemed a natural. Moreover, natural history was everywhere, always. And Texas art never went out of style. Texas A&M Press's problems were not conceptual but financial. How to fund these proposed series?

Former students again provided the answer. This time, individual former students acted as TAMUP's "twelfth man," honoring the tradition that an Aggie is always willing to serve when the school calls.[43] Wardlaw recruited the assistance of the Texas A&M Development Foundation, headed by Robert L. Walker, as well as the Association of Former Students. With John Lindsey's assistance, he began calling upon former students who had the financial wherewithal and the inclination to support the new Texas A&M Press.[44]

In September, 1974, soon after TAMUP officially opened for business, Lindsey brought Wardlaw to Houston to visit Kenneth E. Montague (Class of 1937), president of General Crude Oil Company. They discussed plans for the petroleum history series, which would begin with a pictorial history of Texas oil. Montague was interested and offered to help raise the money required for the series. In November, Wardlaw wrote Montague estimating that about $35,000 would be needed to fund the series initially. This would cover the cost of producing the pictorial history of Texas oil. He described how the revolving fund established with the money would be used to fund subsequent publications in the series. He also explained that Dr. Walter Rundell, Jr., a Texas historian at the University of Maryland, would be a likely author for the first book.[45]

Montague thought it was a good plan. By February, 1975, TAMUP had $25,000 in hand from an anonymous donor (an individual secured by

Montague who chose to remain anonymous, despite appeals from Wardlaw to let his name be used along with Montague's to identify the series) and the promise of an additional $10,000 from Montague. Thus, the Kenneth E. Montague Series in Oil and Business History and an associated revolving fund were established. Walter Rundell began work on *Early Texas Oil: A Photographic History, 1866–1936,* the first book in an attractive and informative series of petroleum history volumes.[46]

Reflecting Wardlaw's great love of the Old Southwest, the press director wanted to create a Texas art series. To initiate this series, he hoped to publish a collection of paintings by Mondel Rogers of Sweetwater, Texas,

> *a brilliant young artist who has produced a splendid series of paintings depicting the great ranches of the High Plains—such ranches as the Matador, the Pitchfork, the JA, the Spur, the XIT, the Masterson, and some forty-five others.*
>
> *There never has been a beautiful art book on the Panhandle and its ranches. This book will bring much pride and joy to the entire region. It will also receive wide circulation in other parts of the country and will bring distinction to the new Texas A&M University Press and to the University itself.*[47]

The search for funding for the Texas art series took Wardlaw and Williams in TAMU's plane first to Aggies in Amarillo and then, on the return flight, to Aggies in Midland. The Aggies in Midland were Joe and Betty Moore, staunch supporters of the university. In 1974, Moore was president of the Association of Former Students, whose motto that year was "More Dough for A&M." Joe Hiram Moore, born in the spring of 1917, was reared in Alvin, southeast of Houston. His father operated four dairies in Alvin, and that meant plenty of activity for Joe Moore and his three brothers and sisters. Despite the onset of the Great Depression, his mother and father insisted that all the children go to college. Joe's oldest brother went to Texas A&M, another followed, and Joe decided that TAMU would suit him, too. He enrolled in 1934, thinking that he would study either agriculture or engineering, but in a short time he had decided that petroleum engineering suited him best. He had some firsthand knowledge of the industry from summer work in the new oil fields being drilled near Alvin. He completed his degree in petroleum engineering in 1938 and decided he needed to know more. He enrolled at the University of Oklahoma to study geology under an "oil finder" geologist.[48]

FIG. 7. *Joe and Betty Moore stand with Frank Wardlaw in front of the old Board of Directors Building about 1975. The first floor of the main building became the Wardlaws' residence, and the second floor held the press offices.*

In the summer of 1939, while visiting his parents, Moore met his future wife. Betty Jane Monthaven had been born in Alvin, but her family had moved to Ohio when she was little and she was in town visiting an aunt. They married in December. Moore finished his master's degree in geology in 1940 and quickly received three job offers. The Depression, at least for petroleum engineers and geologists, was over. He accepted a job in production with Shell Oil Company at the then munificent salary of $135 per month. World War II broke out soon afterward, and Joe, who had resigned his commission after leaving Texas A&M to pursue graduate studies, remained a civilian in an essential war industry. When the war ended, he accepted a job with Fullerton Company (at twice his salary at Shell, he recalled). A few years later, he became an independent geologist.[49]

He and Betty spent the next twenty-five years in Hobbs, New Mexico, exploring for oil, raising three sons, and becoming increasingly active in the affairs of the Association of Former Students. A decision to hold an Aggie Muster in their home led to the organization of a chapter of the Former Students for Hobbs, New Mexico (Northwest Permian Basin A&M Club).[50]

So the timing was right in December, 1974, when Wardlaw, Williams, Haskell Monroe (head of TAMUP's new Faculty Advisory Committee), and Randy Matson, assistant director of the Association of Former Students, "dropped in" on Joe and Betty Moore. Wardlaw very carefully explained his plans for TAMUP and emphasized his interest in publishing a Texas art series that would be introduced with the publication of Mondel Rogers's western ranch scenes. He had samples of Rogers's prints to show.[51]

Joe and Betty Moore were impressed with Wardlaw's sincerity and with Williams's enthusiasm. Betty Moore particularly remembered Jack Williams stressing that, for a university to be great, it had to have a great library and a great press. Joe Moore recalled that, in turn, he "became enthusiastic." The result was that Joe and Betty Moore agreed to give the Texas A&M University Press $75,000 for the Joe and Betty Moore Texas Art Series. The money was placed in a revolving account to fund the publication of Mondel Rogers's *Old Ranches of the Texas Plains* and many subsequent titles.[52] Perhaps more significantly, the Moores became fast friends of the press; many of their friends and acquaintances (among them, noted author James Michener) likewise became supporters of the fledgling publishing house.

Earlier that year, in late September, H. D. Hoese, a professor of biology at the University of Southwestern Louisiana, had visited Wardlaw to propose a guide to the fishes of the Gulf of Mexico, which he would write and illustrate with his colleague Richard Moore. He produced a rough draft of the manuscript and color slides of the illustrations.

When Wardlaw consulted Texas A&M wildlife science professor James Teer and biologists Rezneat Darnell and John McEachran, "a lively two-hour discussion evolved." The book fit perfectly with Wardlaw's interest in natural history publications, but the contents were not in final form. The problem was to determine what form the finished book should take. Too much "scientific apparatus" might overwhelm the lay reader; on the other hand, the inclusion of "full scientific information" would make the book "extremely useful in the classroom as well as in the field."[53] Bookmaking was both a business and an art.

Wardlaw gave Hoese and Moore the "go-ahead" for the book and secured funds from Texas A&M's new Sea Grant program to help cover the cost of producing drawings and color prints. Then he turned to the matter of creating a revolving fund for the publication of a series, as well as the initial title in it. His search led him finally to the Moody Foundation's headquarters in Galveston. In his request for series funding, Wardlaw proposed that the lead volume in the series be Hoese and Moore's *Guide to the Fishes of the Gulf of Mexico*—a title that fit well with Galveston's historic profile as a major Gulf Coast port and a center of Texas' commercial fishing industry. Subsequent titles, he suggested, would include books about edible and medicinal plants of Texas, land forms on the Texas Gulf Coast, Texas wildflowers, and books on mammals, mushrooms, cacti, and crabs.[54] Although it took some time, the foundation agreed to fund the W. L. Moody, Jr., Natural History Series, with a $75,000 contribution.[55] This marked the beginning of TAMUP's very successful and popular Texas natural history guide series.

Thus, in the fall of 1974, during the first months of TAMUP's existence, Wardlaw and his staff, with the help of university administrators and the Association of Former Students, had taken steps that seemed likely to direct the course of the press's scholarly publishing and assure its financial stability. In addition to the critical $200,000 general revolving fund established by the university, Wardlaw had succeeded in creating four specialized revolving funds for the publication of book series using money from outside the university: the $75,000 Joe and Betty Moore Texas Art Series revolving fund; a $75,000 Association of Former Students Centennial Series revolving fund; a $35,000 Montague Petroleum History Series fund; and a $75,000 W. L. Moody, Jr., Natural History Series fund. More such funds—for publications in architecture, photography, and the environment—were under development.

Much of the work of a university press cannot be reckoned in terms of finances or even sales volume. The key element is what Wardlaw called "integrity." Perhaps the best analysis of this integrity was made by the author of the first book actually to come off the presses for Texas A&M University Press. The author was Elizabeth A. H. John, and her book was a history,

Storms Brewed in Other Men's Worlds: The Confrontation of Indians, Spanish, and French in the Southwest, 1540–1795.

Growing up in southeastern Oklahoma, Elizabeth Ann Harper noticed that every spring, when farmers along the Red River plowed their fields, "incredible quantities of artifacts"—Indian and European—were revealed. As a student at the Oklahoma College for Women, she began to study these artifacts in earnest. Her childhood interest led eventually to a Ph.D. in history at the University of Oklahoma, where she studied under Max Moorehead, a distinguished Latin American historian.

In graduate school, she met and married Peter John, a math student specializing in the newly developing field of statistics. He accepted a position at the University of New Mexico. While Elizabeth's energy soon was diverted to raising two children, her interest in the collision of American Indian and European cultures was sharpened by constant exposure to Pueblo and Spanish cultural confluence in New Mexico.[56]

Eventually John revised her dissertation to focus more on the Indian aspect of the European-Amerindian collision and in 1971 submitted her manuscript to the University of Texas Press.[57] Frank Wardlaw was "stunned by the size" of the manuscript; it needed to be shortened and reorganized. John shortened it and resubmitted. This time, Wardlaw said he liked the work but could not at the time publish it because the press's finances were constrained. He thought she should go ahead and seek another publisher. Then, on New Year's Day, 1974, Elizabeth John read in the *Austin American-Statesman* that Wardlaw planned to leave the University of Texas Press to go to Texas A&M University. Shortly thereafter, Wardlaw called to tell her that he was going to begin a press in College Station and that he wanted *Storms* to be the new press's very first book.[58]

John was thrilled but cautious and asked Llerena Friend, archivist at the Bexar Collection, what she thought about publishing with TAMUP. Friend told her that wherever Frank Wardlaw was would be the place to publish. With a freelance copyeditor (Graham Blackstock) and designer (Jo Alice Downs), work on the book began long before Wardlaw arrived in College Station.

John believed that the vital ingredient in the beginning and development of the new press was the director's (and the press's) integrity. Wardlaw, she said, cared about his authors. He coaxed and nursed them along. He had

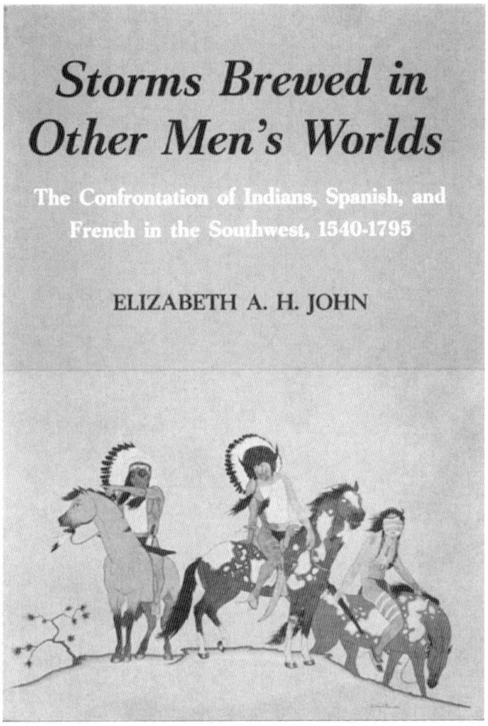

FIG. 8. Storms Brewed in Other Men's Worlds: The Confrontation of Indians, Spanish, and French in the Southwest, 1540–1795, *by historian Elizabeth A. H. John, was one of the first two books published by the fledgling Texas A&M University Press. Both books arrived at the press offices on September 2, 1975.* Storms Brewed *became a classic by which other works of Southwestern history have been judged.*

enormous patience and persistence. He placed great faith in his authors, and they reciprocated by producing their best work. Sometimes he created an author where none existed previously.[59] In effect, Wardlaw and TAMUP entered into a pact with each author that all involved would do their very best to write and publish the best book of which they were professionally capable.

By the close of the fall of 1974, TAMUP had seven books, the Schiwetz art portfolio, and the centennial postcard series scheduled for publication in

1975. John's *Storms Brewed in Other Men's Worlds* would be followed by the two-volume *A Centennial History of Texas A&M University, 1876–1976; Texas A&M University: A Pictorial History, 1876–1867; Buck Schiwetz' Aggieland: A Portfolio of Eight Scenes from Texas A&M University;* and four other books.

One of those books, *The Grasses of Texas,* by Frank Gould, reflected Texas A&M's expertise in agriculture and ranching and fit nicely with Wardlaw's effort to create a series of books in natural history. When Wardlaw arrived on the campus, the book was being prepared for publication by the Texas Agricultural Experiment Station. Wardlaw reimbursed the station for expenses incurred thus far, and the book was published under the press's imprint. Illustrated with precise line drawings by Valloo Kapadia, it proved to be one of the most important and definitive works on the subject, meeting the exacting standards of the scientific community while being of great value to ranchers, environmentalists, and naturalists.[60]

Another book combining the genres of art and natural history was a collection of color photographs of the Texas Hill Country by photographer Jim Bones. A narrative by John Graves, one of the state's best-known writers, accompanied the pictures. *Texas Heartland: A Hill Country Year* is an excellent example of a "book made by Wardlaw" through his encouragement of authors and artists. The book examines in photographs and text the changing seasons and the cycles of nature in one of Texas' most picturesque regions.[61]

The two other books that were "in press" in the fall of 1974 and scheduled for publication in 1975 addressed historical issues of particular relevance to Texas and the Southwest. One of these was a short essay originally presented by Frank E. Vandiver at the Southern Historical Association's annual meeting. Haskell Monroe alerted Wardlaw to the topic of Vandiver's talk several weeks before the presentation. As it happened, Vandiver was an old friend who, since joining the faculty at Rice University in 1955, had achieved distinction as a southern historian, writer, and lecturer. "This ('The Southwest—South or West?') is an intriguing title," wrote Wardlaw, "and I know you will make the most of it. Perhaps you already have other plans for your speech, but if it isn't committed for publication elsewhere, we wonder if the idea of issuing it in a small book here might appeal to you?"[62]

It did. The result was a fascinating study and commentary, *The Southwest: South or West?* The relationship between Vandiver and Wardlaw intensified

FIG. 9. *The definitive* Grasses of Texas *(1975), by Frank W. Gould, helped to establish the press's reputation as a publisher of books in the natural sciences. The book's delicate pen-and-ink illustrations, such as this one of burrograss by Valloo Kapadia, demonstrate the beauty possible in fine technical illustration. Courtesy Lucile Gould Bridges*

with publication of Vandiver's two-volume *Black Jack: The Life and Times of John J. Pershing* in 1977. Finally, in September, 1981, Vandiver would become president of Texas A&M University, and the press would report directly to him.

Another title important for the region's history and self-concept was a diary and field notes of the campaigns of the Texas Revolution, kept by José Enrique de la Peña, an officer with the invading army of Santa Anna. De la Peña participated in the entire campaign from the Alamo to San Jacinto. The text was being translated by Carmen Perry. Even before publication, Wardlaw described *With Santa Anna in Texas: A Personal Narrative of the Revolution* as "startling," a "must" for Texas history buffs.[63] De la Peña's account reported the capture and execution of the legendary Davy Crockett and several other Texian defenders, challenging the version of the Alamo's fall that Texas schoolchildren had learned for more than a hundred years. The furor—and fury—this account unleashed would reflare periodically for years to come, resulting in an expanded version with a new introduction by James E. Crisp in 1997. But that lay in the future. And in 1975, all was future.

Seven books for 1975 seemed like a strong beginning, but it was not enough. In an article written by Charlotte Whelan in November, 1974, for the *Houston Post,* Wardlaw announced that "we will have 12 books on our list for 1976 (most of them already in development at the press), and 20 in '77. We really have to get up to 20 pretty soon. Overhead can eat you up with fewer than 20 books."[64]

The "considerable thought" that Wardlaw had given to this new press extended considerably beyond 1977. The fall of 1974, by any reckoning, was an incredible beginning. Although no books were yet in print, TAMUP was a reality. Already it had a history closely intertwined with the experiences of its director and staff, with the traditions of Texas A&M University and its Association of Former Students, and with its authors and associates and the university's administration and faculty.

The tie between the faculty and the press was strengthened by the creation of a Faculty Advisory Committee, set up according to the guidelines of the Association of American University Presses. While admitting that "such committees can become damned nuisances," Wardlaw believed that a press should not operate without a faculty advisory committee:[65]

FIG. 10. *Gen. John J. Pershing, the focus of Frank E. Vandiver's two-volume* Black Jack: The Life and Times of John J. Pershing. *This future National Book Award runner-up was published by the press in 1977 when Vandiver was provost at Rice University. Frank Wardlaw, in order to encourage Vandiver to bring his lengthy manuscript to A&M, joked that the press would publish it "by the pound."*

> *Faculties seldom are really behind their university presses because each faculty member has a different idea as to what we should be doing, usually seen in the light of their individual interests. Our biggest job is to persuade our own administrations and our faculties that we do indeed play a vital role in the effort to advance knowledge and that they would be in sorry shape without us.*[66]

A faculty advisory committee served many purposes. It provided a credible body to review and evaluate manuscripts and book projects, and it served as a medium for the diffusion of information about the press to the general faculty. Moreover, its members could assist in procuring publishable manuscripts from the university community and from colleagues elsewhere.

In 1975, Wardlaw, since he was not yet acquainted with most of the A&M faculty, asked President Williams to appoint the press's first Faculty Advisory Committee. Williams appointed a selection of both young and more mature faculty members representing the disciplines of the university. He also asked Haskell Monroe, professor of history and dean of faculties, to chair the committee. Wardlaw kept Monroe closely advised on the development of the press and relied upon members of the advisory committee to assist in the review and evaluation of manuscripts under consideration for publication. Committee members also assisted in directing manuscripts to authorities and scholars throughout the United States for peer review.[67] Thus, the Faculty Advisory Committee, like the revolving funds, became a significant factor in the press's continuing development. It would be particularly instrumental in establishing the press's scholarly credibility and integrity.

All of this, compressed into a few months, formed part of what Wardlaw termed "the beginning." These months and these activities set the tone and direction of the Texas A&M University Press for the years to follow. Still, this was only a beginning. Much remained to be done. Selling books was as important as producing them. Now, with books "in press," it was time to begin a marketing and sales program. It was also time to expand the editorial department, in order to be able to manage the editing and production of the next twelve manuscripts already identified for publication in 1976, and the twenty or more that were to follow in 1977.

Wardlaw asked Donald A. Collins, who had worked in business at the University of Texas Press, if he would be interested in joining him as business manager of TAMUP. Collins accepted with enthusiasm. Wardlaw welcomed him to the team and promised to "do all I can to keep you moving forward as the size and complexity of the job grows."[68]

At the annual meeting of the Association of American University Presses in June, 1975, Wardlaw found the person he had been seeking to fill the position of associate editor. "His name is Noel Parsons, and he is editor of the staff of the University of Illinois Press," he wrote in a letter to University Vice President John C. Calhoun, adding, "we have been extremely fortunate in our selection of key personnel thus far; they are all competent, hardworking professionals who delight in their work."[69]

Less than a year old, TAMUP could boast of a proven director, a strong staff who worked as a team and delighted in their work, and an involved, supportive faculty. The new press's assets also included a $200,000 unrestricted revolving fund established by the university, three revolving funds established and already capitalized for a total of $260,000 in gift money, and two additional funds promised and anticipated to total $125,000. Despite prevailing high inflation, the Texas economy, based as it was upon agriculture, cattle, petroleum, petrochemicals, and diversified industries, was uniquely strong. This augured well for future funding and for regional book sales. A further "decided plus factor" was the almost fanatical loyalty of Texas Aggies to their alma mater: "They already think of us as 'their' press." Wardlaw, himself a sports lover, was gratified that, in a recent edition of the alumni magazine, the *Texas Aggie,* "the first three books of the press got top billing over the undefeated football team and the funeral of Reveille, the school mascot."[70]

Texas Heartland: A Hill Country Year, *with photographs by Jim Bones and an introduction by John Graves, was the other of the first two books published by the Press. Together, these publications established a precedent for fine books of photography and art as well as the best of scholarship.*

The first book in the Joe and Betty Moore Texas Art Series was Old Ranches of the Texas Plains, *by Sweetwater artist Mondel Rogers. It combined the Press's interests in Texas art and the state's western heritage. This painting of W. H. Gray's LS Ranch headquarters is entitled "Peerage on the Plains."*

As artist-in-residence at Texas A&M from 1974 to 1977, E. M. "Buck" Schiwetz painted a series of scenes, past and present, from the A&M campus. This print, "Old Main," was one of eight prints in the portfolio Buck Schiwetz' Aggieland *(1976).*

The W. L. Moody, Jr., Natural History Series received a powerful launching with publication in 1977 of the field guide Fishes of the Gulf of Mexico. *The book is still in print in its second edition. This is a squirrelfish, photographed by Farley Sonnier.*

(right) In 1977 the Press staff cooperated with the Texas Parks and Wildlife Department to produce Texas Wildlife: Photographs from Texas Parks & Wildlife Magazine. *The book was the first volume in the Louise Lindsey Merrick Texas Environment Series and established a collegial working relationship with Parks and Wildlife and other state agencies.*

In press at the time of the fire was The Texas Gulf Coast: Interpretations by Nine Artists *(1979), an anthology of Texas art collected and edited by Frank Wardlaw. The book was introduced by* Houston Post *newspaper columnist Leon Hale, and it included a foreword by* Post *arts editor Ann Holmes. This painting is "End of Jetty," by Dan Wingren.*

(left) The second volume in the Louise Lindsey Merrick Texas Environment Series, The Natural World of the Texas Big Thicket, *by photographer-writer Blair Pittman, combined a description of the controversial establishment of the Big Thicket National Preserve with beautiful full-color photographs. This one is of iris leaves and water-shield.*

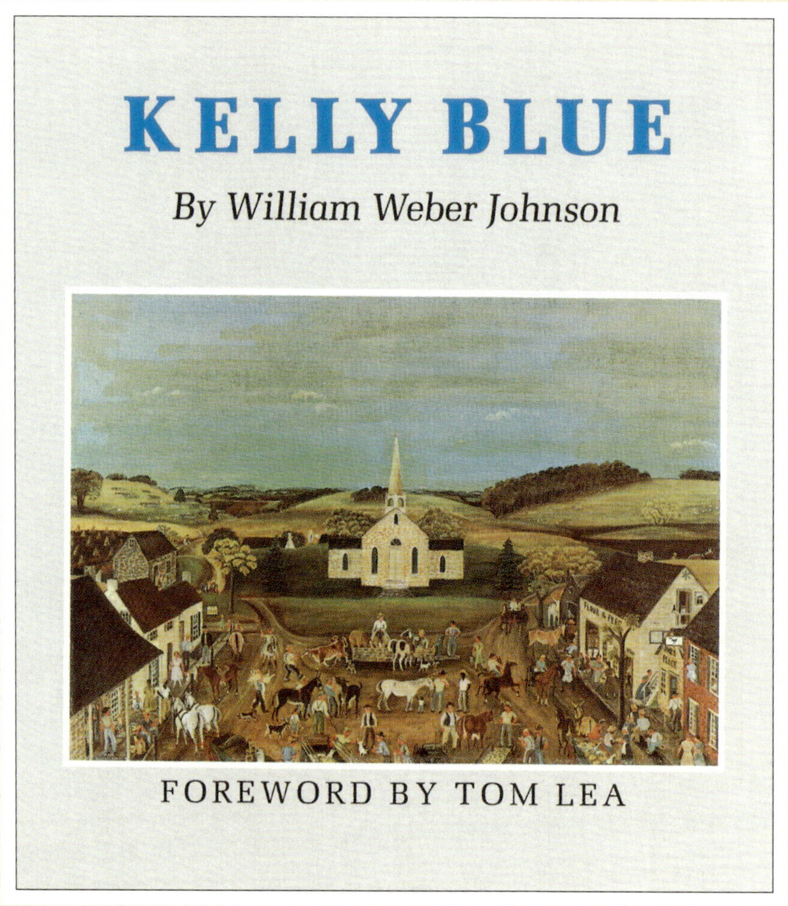

Another art book published in 1979 was the delightful Kelly Blue, *written by William Weber Johnson and with a foreword by Tom Lea. The book told the story of the life of Texas naïve artist H. O. "Cowboy" Kelly and presented a selection of his work. This painting is titled "More Good People."*

(right) Landscapes of Texas *was published in the Louise Lindsey Merrick Series in 1980 in cooperation with the staff of* Texas Highways Magazine. *Page after page of beautiful landscape photography from every section of the state have made it a perennial favorite of Texans everywhere, and it has become the Press's all-time best-seller. This scene from the Big Bend country was captured by Highways Department staff photographer Jack Lewis.*

Frank Wardlaw continued to compile and edit collections of art for the Joe and Betty Moore Texas Art Series after his retirement. In 1981 the Press published The Texas Hill Country: Interpretations by Thirteen Artists, *introduced by A. C. Greene and with a foreword by John Palmer Leeper. Shown here is "Stream," by William Hoey.*

Baytown nature photographer and writer John Tveten joined the Press's family of authors in 1982 with his book Coastal Texas: Water, Land, and Wildlife. *With its coordinated text and color photographs, the book is a celebration of the diversity and beauty of the Texas Gulf Coast.*

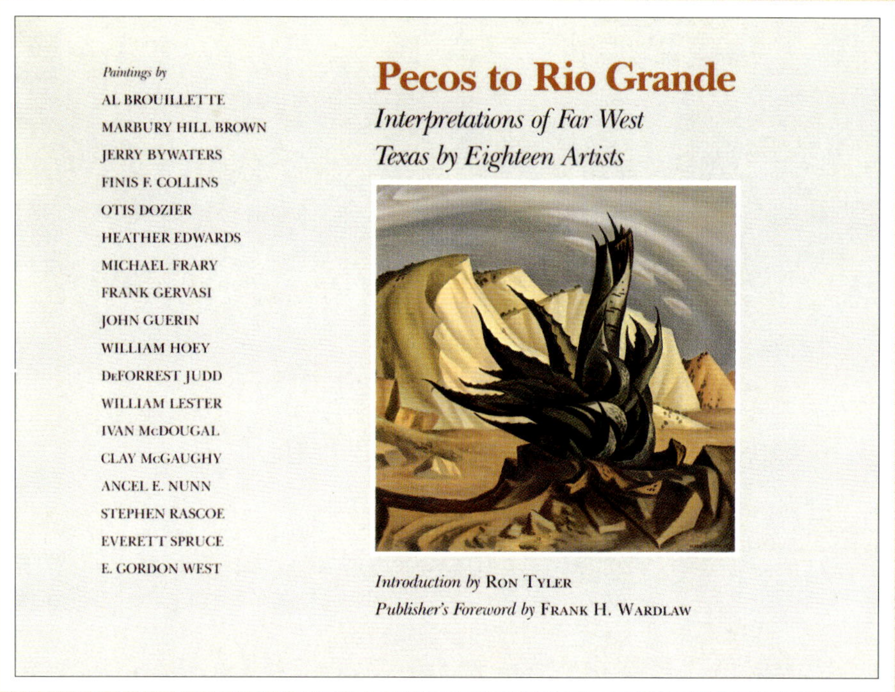

Frank Wardlaw's last compilation of Texas art, published in 1983, was Pecos to Rio Grande: Interpretations of Far West Texas by Eighteen Artists, *number six in the Joe and Betty Moore Texas Art Series. This painting is "Shafter—A Quicksilver Mining Town," by Jerry Bywaters.*

Rick Bass's first book, The Deer Pasture, *was published by the Press in 1985. This collection of stories about Bass's family, their relationships, and the meaning their deer lease had as a gathering place, was illustrated by the author's wife-to-be, Elizabeth Hughes.*

The John H. Lindsey Building, completed and dedicated in 1983, is the home of Texas A&M University Press. This watercolor is by Design Manager Mary Ann Jacob.

Texas in Bloom: Photographs from Texas Highways Magazine, *published in 1984, was another cooperative effort with the Texas Department of Highways and Public Transportation. The book's introduction was by Glen Evans, and the foreword was by Lady Bird Johnson.*

In 1984 the Press published its second art book featuring a single artist. Frank Reaugh: Painter to the Longhorns, *with an introduction by Donald Weismann, compiles a large collection of the lovely pastels and paintings of one of the deans of Texas art. This pastel, "Morning Light," is typical of Reaugh's work.*

A Flying Tiger's Diary, *by former Flying Tiger Charles R. Bond, Jr., and Terry H. Anderson, has been one of the Press's most successful military history books. Published in the Centennial Series of the Association of Former Students, it was reprinted for the fifth time in 1996. This cover-art painting by Terry Pyles illustrates Bond's first air victory in the skies over Burma in early 1942.*

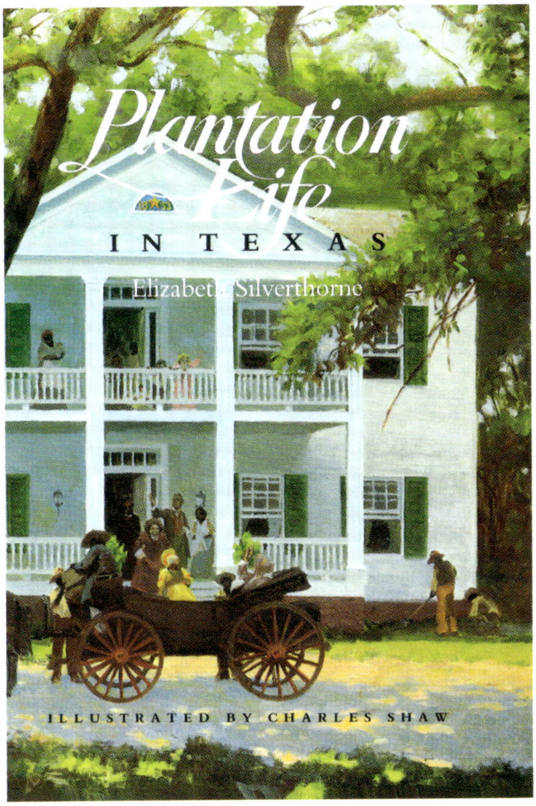

With encouragement from James Michener and funding from Clayton Williams, Jr., the Press initiated the Clayton Wheat Williams Texas Life Series in 1986 with the publication of Elizabeth Silverthorne's Plantation Life in Texas. *The book was illustrated with a cover painting and drawings by Charles Shaw.*

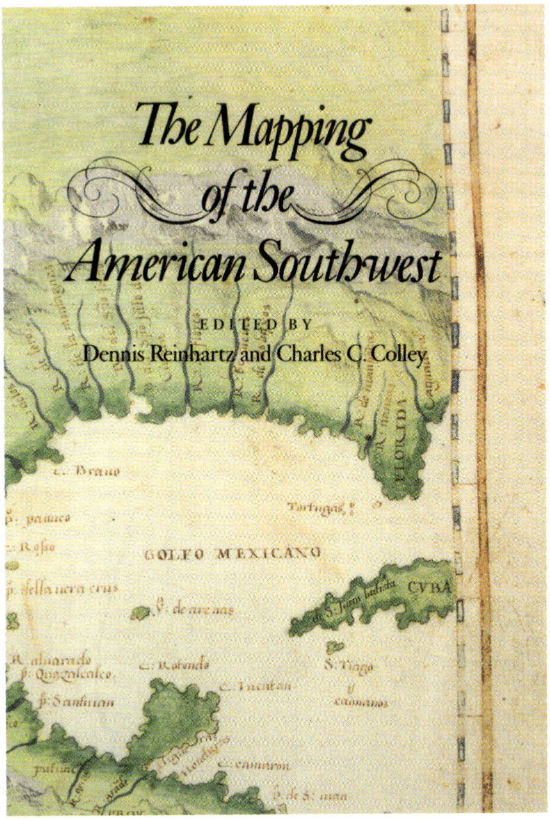

Some of the Press's most beautiful books have been collaborative efforts with other institutions. An example of this is The Mapping of the American Southwest, *edited by Dennis Reinhartz and Charles C. Colley, published with Special Collections of the University of Texas at Arlington Library in 1987. The map on this cover is from a portolan atlas, probably drawn by Battista Agnese about 1557.*

Texas nature writer Howard Peacock edited The Nature of Texas: A Feast of Native Beauty from Texas Highways Magazine *in 1990 for the Louise Lindsey Merrick Texas Environment Series. This photograph from the book, of a question mark butterfly, is by Geyata Ajilvsgi, who also wrote* Wildflowers of the Big Thicket, East Texas, and Western Louisiana, *which the Press published in 1979.*

The love of things Western continues, as shown by the popularity of the Press's book Cowboy Spurs and Their Makers *(1991), by Jane Pattie and with a foreword by Don Worcester. This cover illustration [photograph], originally published in* Persimmon Hill *magazine of the Cowboy Hall of Fame in Oklahoma City, shows spurs made by Bob Boone [Adolph Bayers].*

(below) Artist Tom Lea, who designed the Press's pressmark and illustrated a number of books published by the Press, became the subject of a retrospective in 1989 with the publication of The Art of Tom Lea, *compiled by Kathleen G. Hjerter and with an introduction by William Weber Johnson. This work is "The Year It Rained," painted by Lea in 1975.*

A happy convergence of events led to the publication of Lighthouses of Texas *in 1991. Historian T. Lindsay Baker wrote the text, Houston artist Harold Phenix illustrated the book with watercolors, and the National Parks Service provided funding with a grant through the Texas Historical Commission. The cover illustration is Sabine Pass lighthouse.*

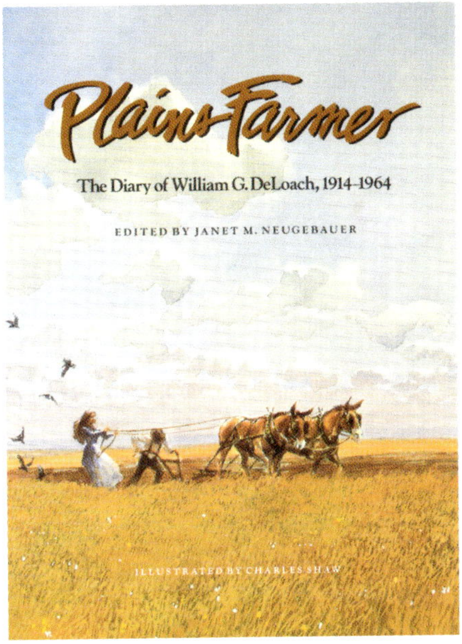

Plains Farmer: The Diary of William G. DeLoach, 1914–1964, *edited by Janet Neugebauer, presented fifty years of daily life of a High Plains cotton farmer as a volume in the Clayton Wheat Williams Texas Life Series. Like* Plantation Life in Texas, *this book was illustrated by Charles Shaw.*

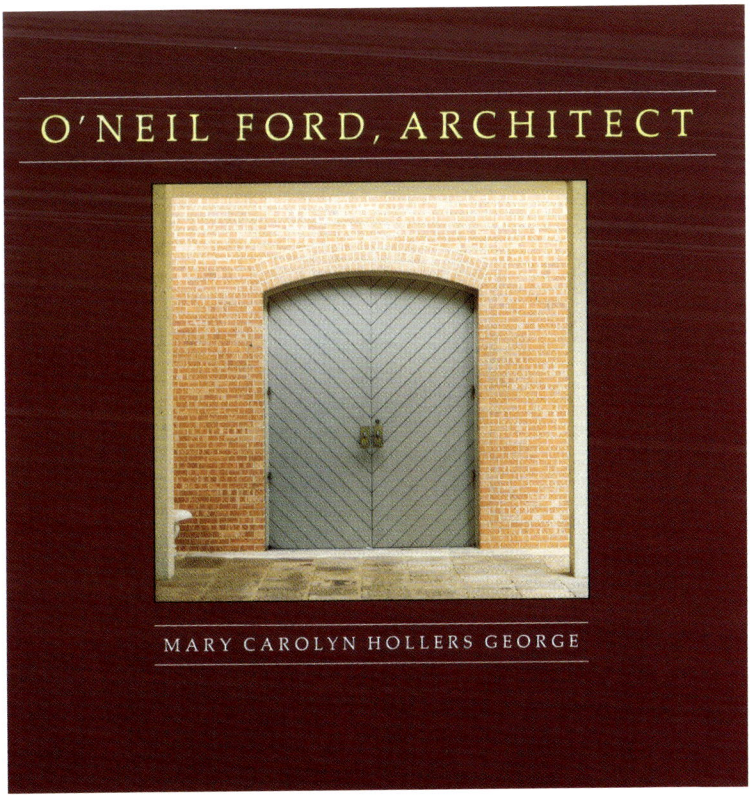

San Antonio architect O'Neil Ford was one of the leading designers in Texas from the mid-1930s through the 1970s. This 1992 book, by Mary Carolyn Hollars George, and with photographs by W. Eugene George, presents Ford's life and work in a beautiful 11x11-inch format.

When the Newsweek *magazine staff went looking for a publisher of their account of the 1992 presidential campaign, they came to Texas A&M University Press. The result,* Quest for the Presidency 1992, *by Peter Goldman, Thomas M. DeFrank, Mark Miller, Andrew Murr, and Tom Mathews, was published in 1994.*

Karen Carr illustrated the book Lone Star Dinosaurs, *by paleontologist Louis Jacobs. This 1995 book caught the wave of renewed interest in dinosaurs inspired by the movie* Jurassic Park, *and it brought to life, in effect, the story of those great creatures that once roamed the land that is now Texas.*

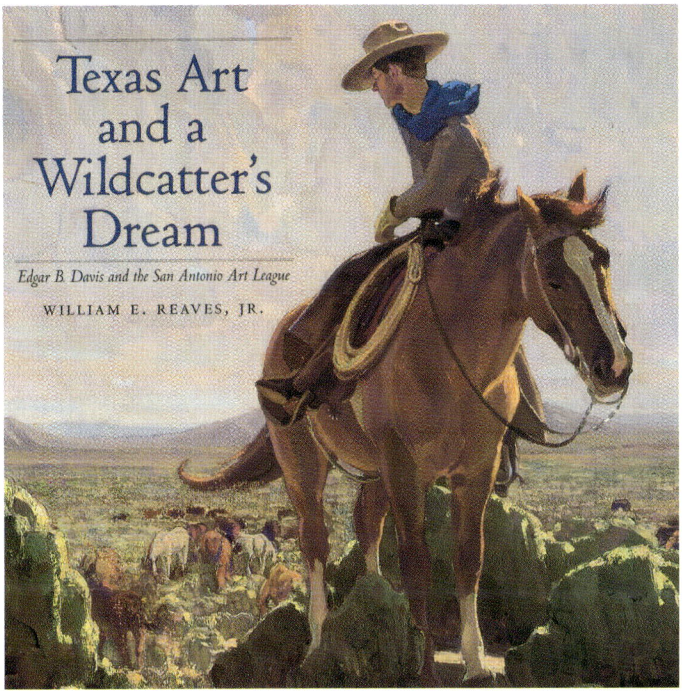

At the time of publication of this history, the Press continues to intensify its publication program. Texas Art and a Wildcatter's Dream, *by William E. Reaves, Jr., published in the spring of 1998 in the Joe and Betty Moore Texas Art Series, tells the story of oilman Edgar B. Davis, the San Antonio Art League, and a series of art competitions that helped develop Texas artistic trends. The cover painting is "The Horse Wrangler," by W. Herbert Dunton.*

The Press prepares to enter the twenty-first century with a new focus on the history of flight and space exploration. In anticipation of that direction, the Press issued in fall of 1998 Planetary Astronomy: From Ancient Times to the Third Millennium, *by NASA astronomer Ronald A. Schorn.*

Also in fall 1998 the Press published volume six in the Charles and Elizabeth Prothro Texas Photography Series. Journeys into Czech Moravian Texas *studies, in photographs and text, the Texans of Czech heritage and their exemplification of the multicultural richness of the state.*

In the spring of 1999 the Press published its second book by Alexander F. Skutch, noted author of more than twenty-five books on birds and nature. Trogons, Laughing Falcons, and Other Neotropical Birds *followed Skutch's nationally reviewed* The Minds of Birds *(1996) on the Press's list. This cover art is by illustrator Dana Gardner.*

Chapter 2

AIR, EARTH, FIRE, AND WATER

The logo that Tom Lea designed for the Texas A&M University Press depicts air, earth, fire, and water—the basic elements, as the ancient Greeks understood the cosmos. Denoting the dispersed intellectual cosmos of the modern world, the logo suggests that today energies are focused and released through ideas and expressions captured on the printed page. The elements depicted by the logo proved to be much more than abstractions in the formative years of the Texas A&M University Press.

A scholarly publisher's basic constituents are its people—the director and the staff. Whatever a press is or becomes is largely a product of the distinctive human elements that create and develop it. These elements can be external as well as internal, however. University administrators such as President Jack Williams and former students such as John Lindsey, Joe Moore, Buck Schiwetz, and Kenneth Montague have left a powerful imprint upon TAMUP. So, of course, have its directors and staff.

Noel Parsons joined TAMUP in September, 1975. A native Oklahoman, Parsons had graduated from the University of Oklahoma, served four years in the U.S. Air Force, and then returned to Oklahoma on the GI Bill to pursue a master's degree in journalism. A fellowship program took him to the University of Oklahoma Press—his first exposure to the unique niche that university presses occupy in the world of journalism and publishing.[1]

In July, 1975, while working at the University of Illinois Press, Parsons was interviewed by Wardlaw for a position at the new press. It was what

Parsons recalled in 1997 as a "memorable" talk.[2] Wardlaw first offered him a cigar and a scotch. Parsons wasn't a cigar smoker or much of a drinker, but he responded to the graciousness of his host and accepted both. Puffing on the cigar, Parsons choked and gasped his way through the interview, attempting to hide his distress while Wardlaw explained his plans for Texas A&M University Press. Wardlaw then invited him to come to College Station to visit the press and the Texas A&M campus.[3]

The next month, the Wardlaws, in their "Aggie Suite" apartment, hosted the Parsons family. Together with Margaret Ingram, Ray Grimaila, and Gayla Christiansen, Frank and Rosemary showed the visitors the town and campus. Parsons was most impressed by the fact that Wardlaw took him to meet and be interviewed by University President Jack Williams. Clearly, the administration strongly supported the new publishing house.[4]

Parsons joined Wardlaw's growing team on September 1, 1975, the day before the press's first two books arrived from the bindery.[5] This was the beginning of TAMUP's second year in business, in the course of which sixteen books were published.

Ingram and Parsons did all the copyediting. Wardlaw, with help from Ingram, concentrated on acquisitions. Grimaila handled design and composition. Don Collins managed warehousing, packing, shipping, and distribution, while Christiansen took care of the other details inherent in bookmaking.

The first two books arrived from the bindery on September 2, 1975. They were Elizabeth A. H. John's *Storms Brewed in Other Men's Worlds: The Confrontation of Indians, Spanish, and French in the Southwest, 1540–1795;* and Jim Bones and John Graves's *Texas Heartland: A Hill Country Year.* It was an exciting beginning. The staff became a close-knit group, meeting weekly to formally discuss projects under way but interacting constantly.[6]

Staff members formed part of the Wardlaw family, a family which came to extend throughout the campus, the community, the state, and beyond. Wardlaw wrote to a friend with the Association of American University Presses: "I have a wonderful staff. There are only seven of us, not counting part-time clerical and shipping room help, but they are all the best a director could hope for. We work well and happily as a team. Everybody pitches in and does a bit of everything. It is all great good fun."[7] For Wardlaw, publishing was a lifestyle that could not be broken down into the separate components of work and play.

Parsons remembers that, while publishing was a team enterprise, the director was clearly the team leader. Wardlaw knew what needed to be done. The weekly meetings of the press staff were inclined to be "informational" meetings in which he shared that information with his staff.[8] Wardlaw worked tirelessly and tended to do things himself rather than delegate tasks to others. This was easy for him to do, since, for him, publishing was a total commitment encompassing both work and play.

Wardlaw's personal style was so engaging that others quickly became enmeshed in his efforts. This meant that the TAMUP publishing team extended far beyond the physical confines of the press. Wardlaw and the new press had the support of A&M's faculty, former students, and administration.[9]

An important branch of the extended TAMUP family was the Faculty Advisory Committee (FAC). At the beginning, Wardlaw asked President Williams to appoint a faculty committee that would be broadly representative of the university and would serve the press as an advisory editorial body. Chaired by Dr. Haskell Monroe, the first FAC consisted of George F. Carter (geography), Elenor Cox (biology), Rezneat Darnell (oceanography), Eirik G. Furubotn (economics), Graham Horsley (environmental design), Jerome M. Loving (English), Alvin A. Price (veterinary physiology and pharmacology), V. Thomas Rhyne (electrical engineering), Robert P. Strawser (accounting), James G. Teer (wildlife and fisheries science), and Philip T. West (educational administration). No book could be published by TAMUP without the FAC's approval. The committee soon became an integral part of the bookmaking process. Moreover, its chair, Haskell Monroe, became a most effective emissary for the new press among faculty, administrators, former students, and prospective authors.

The publishing process began with solicitation or receipt of manuscripts and book proposals from prospective authors. The proposals or manuscripts then were screened by the director and editor, who examined the proposals from the dual perspectives of quality and marketability. A manuscript that offered possibilities was referred to outside readers who were considered authorities on the specific topic. If the readers' reports were favorable, these reports, along with the recommendations of the staff, were presented to an ad hoc subcommittee of the Faculty Advisory Committee (selected because of particular expertise in the subject matter of the manuscript). If subcom-

FIG. 11. *The Advisory Council of Texas A&M University Press met for the first time in November 1978. In attendance at that meeting were,* front row, left to right: *Lloyd Lyman, H. C. Heldenfels, Susan McAshan, Betty Moore, and William O. Trogdon;* second row, left to right: *Haskell Monroe, Sterling C. Evans, John H. Lindsey, Frank Wardlaw, John Caple, Ford D. Albritton, and Jack K. Williams.*

mittee members desired to do so, they could review the manuscript independently. Ordinarily the ad hoc FAC subcommittee approved publication following a lively discussion, occasionally suggested revisions, and infrequently recommended that a manuscript not be published.[10] The process afforded director and staff considerable leverage in the selection and review of manuscripts. It also provided for broad peer review, exposed possible problems or issues related to publication, and assured the quality of TAMUP publications.

Wardlaw explained the philosophy behind faculty advisory committee review in a letter to Charles E. Cunningham, then editor-in-chief of the University of Washington Press:

> *I wouldn't want to operate without a faculty advisory committee of some kind. The faculty of a university should be involved in some significant way in the program of a Press. I think that basically they should control the imprint and that the director and editors should have to demonstrate to them that each book submitted*

> *for acceptance is worthy to bear that imprint. Also, it is frequently well to be able to share the onus with a faculty committee when rejecting a manuscript submitted by a member of your own faculty.*[11]

To be sure, some publishable book manuscripts never made it to the review stage, because the director had decided to publish only in certain areas—those funded as a series, "the environmental sciences and . . . subjects of regional interest to Texas and the Southwest, with some excursions into other fields."[12] Regularly Wardlaw referred to his successor in Austin prospective authors whose work (on Latin America and Mexico, for example) seemed more appropriate for the list of the University of Texas Press.

One work that Wardlaw declined to review was a book manuscript being written in 1974 by Dr. Michael DeBakey and a Russian colleague on pioneering developments in heart transplant and cardiovascular surgery. Despite the fact that the book would have been a coup for the press, Wardlaw stated, "We do not intend to publish medical books and don't have the know-how to do so successfully. . . . I have resolved never to publish a book unless I know we can publish it effectively."[13] Establishing the credibility of a press often had as much to do with what that press declined to publish as with the titles it did publish.

Establishing credibility also involved promotion and advertising. Wardlaw actively sought to bond TAMUP to the Association of Former Students. Each publication in the Centennial Series bore the legend "The Centennial Series of The Association of Former Students of Texas A&M University." Wardlaw explained to Buck Weirus and Jerry Cooper, editor of the university's alumni magazine, the *Texas Aggie,* that TAMUP would like to sell its publications on a regular basis through the magazine. Cooper enthusiastically agreed to feature Texas A&M Press in future issues. Wardlaw believed that the remarkable loyalty of Aggies to their alma mater would cause many of them to want to buy the press's books, particularly those books that dealt with Texas.[14] The Association of Former Students, the *Texas Aggie,* and TAMUP soon established enduring relationships.

The Texas A&M Development Foundation was another critical component in Wardlaw's efforts to create a durable infrastructure for the new publishing house. Writing to the foundation's director, Robert L. Walker, in July, 1975, Wardlaw explained that he was "eager to get the new Texas A&M

University Press off the ground in the best possible way"—not only for the sake of the press, but also "because of the additional national and international prestige that will come to the University because of this book publication program." He explained that, because the A&M Press imprint was a new one, "completely unknown to the book world," it would take extra effort to promote the publications and achieve recognition for TAMUP.[15]

Wardlaw believed that the new press offered the university an unusual opportunity to correct the prevailing "false impression" that Texas A&M was just a "cow college." While any large campaign of institutional advertising would be viewed as self-serving and hence would be largely unproductive, advertisements for Texas A&M University Press books would enhance the university's name throughout the nation and the world.

He suggested that, if the Development Foundation would raise $10,000 for each of the next two years, to be used for advertising TAMUP books, the benefits for both the university and the press would be great. The following month, President Williams informed Wardlaw that Kenneth Montague, chair of the TAMU Development Foundation (who had helped to create the press's Kenneth E. Montague Series in Oil and Business History), had approved $20,000 for the press over the next two years for "extra advertising to enable the press to make its imprint better known nationally."[16]

Wardlaw continued to tap TAMU's seemingly inexhaustible resources for continuing support. In January, 1976, one of A&M's former students anonymously donated an initial $50,000 to fund the Texas A&M University Economics Series. The first publication in the series, *Regulating Competition in Oil: Government Intervention in the U.S. Refining Industry, 1948–1975*, by E. Anthony Copp, appeared in 1976. Copp's study was in part a response to the embargo by the Organization of Petroleum Exporting Countries (OPEC) on the shipment of oil from member nations to the United States, Japan, and Europe. The OPEC embargo escalated the price of crude oil from two dollars to thirty-two dollars per barrel; the resulting financial crisis was one of the reasons Wardlaw had believed 1975 was a particularly bad year to create a new university press. Copp, a manager for energy and resource development with Salomon Brothers of New York, believed that, because energy-use allocations were so heavily weighted by government planning, independent and major oil companies in America were likely to lose actual or potential market power to governments, both foreign and domestic. OPEC's rise to world economic power required the development of a new national energy policy.[17]

The second book in the series, *Freedom in Constitutional Contract: Perspectives of a Political Economist,* by James M. Buchanan, published in 1977, was one of many books that established Buchanan as a leading contemporary free-market economist. In 1986, he received the Nobel Prize for his contributions to modern political economics. TAMUP published two more books by Buchanan and, in 1990, David Riesman's *The Political Economy of James Buchanan,* which examined Buchanan's career. The Texas A&M University Economics Series complemented the programs of A&M's outstanding economics department.[18]

Wardlaw again turned to the Development Foundation for assistance in securing a grant to fund a military history series that would reflect Texas A&M's military tradition. The university had been a major supplier of men and officers for the nation's armed forces since the Spanish-American War of 1898.[19] Of the nearly twenty thousand Aggies who served in World War II, fourteen thousand served as officers, and twenty-nine of these held the rank of general. Gen. Omar Bradley had told the 1950 graduating class that the men of Texas A&M University "can stand up to any men in the world and compare favorably their education and training for leadership—leadership in the pursuits of peace and, if it comes to war, leadership in battle."[20] A military history series was both logical and necessary.

The series, once funding was found, would be launched with the publication of a monumental two-volume biography of Gen. John J. Pershing, written by Frank E. Vandiver, historian and provost of Rice University. The work would cover Pershing's military career from the Spanish-American War until his death in 1946. "It is bound," Wardlaw explained to Robert Walker, "to attract international attention, to gain wide recognition for the new Texas A&M University Press, and to enhance the reputation of the University itself." In the search for funding for a military history series, Wardlaw also enlisted Wayne Stark, director of the university's Memorial Student Center, whose personal connections to Aggies past and present were many and close.[21] As funding for the series proved elusive, Wardlaw decided to publish Vandiver's book on Pershing using funds from the press's general revolving account. The result was the 1977 publication of *Black Jack: The Life and Times of John J. Pershing,* a finalist in the competition for the 1978 National Book Award and a History Book Club Main Selection.[22] In 1997, *U.S. News & World Report* would cite *Black Jack* as the "definitive" biography of Pershing. It was reprinted in 1999.

In 1986, Weldon E. Rhoades's *Flying MacArthur to Victory* became the first book in the Texas A&M University Military History Series, despite the fact that, at that point, the series still was not underwritten by a special fund. Other books followed, tracing the history of America at war from the Civil War through the Vietnam conflict. The series has included works on the World War I Battle of Verdun, the experiences of American women in the U.S. Navy and Air Force, the trauma of Korea, and the killing fields of Cambodia.

When it came to netting funds for TAMUP, Wardlaw was an expert fisherman who sometimes cast his line in secluded spots where no one else had fished. One of these spots was a bookstore in San Antonio owned and managed by Florence Rosengren. She loved books and, in an older bookseller tradition, selectively provided her customers with titles they wanted to read or should want to read. In February, 1977, Wardlaw wrote to Rosengren, reminding her that, while he was director of the University of Texas Press (UTP), she had introduced him to one of her customers, Elma Dill Russell Spencer, who subsequently gave UTP funds to publish *The Roadside Flowers of Texas* and other works on Texas topics. Later Spencer endowed TAMUP's Elma Dill Russell Spencer Series on the West and Southwest, which was initiated in 1976 with Joe Frantz's *Aspects of the American West: Three Essays.*

"Now, for my new press at Texas A&M," Wardlaw informed Rosengren, "I am seeking similar support for a series of beautiful books on various aspects of the Texas environment." Could she help him find such a person?[23]

Indeed Rosengren could. The press's list soon was buttressed by a $50,000 endowment from Louise Lindsey Merrick of Tyler, Texas, to be used to establish a revolving fund for the publication of books on the Texas environment.[24] In June, 1977, President Williams announced the establishment of the Louise Lindsey Merrick Natural Environment Series: "Throughout the years books published in the Merrick Series will serve to remind Texas of the great richness and variety of their environment and of the necessity to preserve it for future generations."[25]

Wardlaw informed Merrick that the first book scheduled for publication in the series would be *Texas Wildlife: Photographs from Texas Parks and Wildlife Magazine,* the result of a cooperative effort between the Texas A&M University's wildlife sciences department and the highly regarded *Texas Parks and Wildlife* magazine. He wanted to visit in order to thank her personally for everything she had done for TAMUP, but she declined, explaining that she was a semi-invalid and could not tolerate exertion or excitement. Published in 1978, *Texas Wildlife* contained 232 color plates; a preface by James G. Teer, head of A&M's wildlife and fisheries sciences department; and an introduction and narrative by Texas Parks and Wildlife Department officials David Baxter, Ted L. Clark, and John Jefferson.[26]

The revolving funds maintained by sales from the Merrick Natural Environment Series and the W. L. Moody, Jr., Natural History Series have allowed the press to produce such books as, in the Moody series, Frank W. Gould's *Common Texas Grasses: An Illustrated Guide* (which went through five printings within a few years) and David J. Schmidly's *Mammals of Trans-Pecos Texas: Including Big Bend National Park and Guadalupe Mountains National Park;* and, in the Merrick series, Blair Pittman's *The Natural World of the Texas Big Thicket.* Wardlaw's careful thought and intensive effort were producing positive benefits for the new press, the university, and the world of books.

While planning clearly defined the directions TAMUP would take, unplanned and unforeseen events provided the kinds of surprises that make book publishing truly exciting. Such was the case with *The Stolen Steers.* William A. Owens, an author, folklorist, and raconteur with a Texas base and a national following, called Wardlaw's attention to stories being told by Bill Brett and sometimes published in the *Liberty Gazette,* a small newspaper in southeastern Texas: "Bill Brett has been an oil well roughneck and driller, cowhand, ranch foreman, farmer, rancher, deputy sheriff, construction worker, truck driver, and postmaster of Hull, Texas."

Wardlaw responded warmly: "Thank you for your valuable report on Bill Brett's stories. You said exactly what needed to be said in your own inimitable way. Now I must find three people on our committee and campus who will understand. I really want to publish this one."[27] Brett had little formal education and none of the usual credentials of a university press author. His accreditation came from the school of real life and hard knocks. In Brett, Wardlaw had found a "diamond in the rough," underscoring again his uncanny ability to discover the natural talent and regional raw material that together sometimes can produce a book.

In 1977, *The Stolen Steers: A Tale of the Big Thicket* first saw print. Four

FIG. 12. *Bill Brett's classic Texas novel* The Stolen Steers *was published to high acclaim in 1982. Michael Frary illustrated the book with pen-and-ink drawings like the one shown here.*

printings and two decades later, it (like other Brett books) had become a classic of its genre. Owens described it as "the kind of history that gets told but rarely written." Brett had heard this story from a man in southeastern Texas who was in his nineties when he told Brett the tale of a young man who had been laid off his job in the oil fields because of an injury. Down on his luck, the young fellow decided to steal a small herd of cattle. While driving the cattle east, he succumbed to malaria and was nursed back to health by an impoverished black family. "There's no words to describe the cold that a man feels with a malarial chill." When he finally was able to sell his stolen herd, he gave the money to his benefactors, who in turn shared their new wealth with others.[28]

Another early publication was equally remarkable, rich, and spontaneous, but in a wholly different way. *The Junks of Central China,* published in 1976, did not fit into the press's specified subject areas. Why would a landlocked Texas agricultural college publish a book about Chinese boats? This publication reflected both the changing identity of the university and the role that the faculty and administration saw for the press in helping to establish that identity. In September, 1974, the same month in which TAMUP opened its doors, the Spencer Collection of Model Chinese Junks went on display at A&M's Memorial Student Center.

This exhibition had come about because of the long-standing admiration of a professor of geography, Edwin Doran, Jr., for the "junk" collection owned by Joseph E. Spencer, his friend and colleague at the University of California at Los Angeles. Doran, who had been interested in the collection for at least fifteen years, admitted that he had made a nuisance of himself, urging Spencer to put the collection on public display at Texas A&M. Spencer agreed with the nuisance part, noting that "Edwin Doran, being under a spell as to nautical matters . . . for years had been at me about it."

Once Spencer agreed to the display, Doran realized that an illustrated guide "would make the collection more accessible." Vice President for Academic Affairs John C. Calhoun, then very much involved in helping to define Texas A&M's new mission as a Sea Grant college and establishing the Moody College of Marine Sciences and Maritime Resources in Galveston, agreed that an illustrated guide to Chinese junks would be an appropriate publication for A&M's new press. He located the university funds needed to publish the book.[29] Wardlaw was delighted.

FIG. 13. *In the early 1970s, Professor J. E. Spencer gave the Geography Department at Texas A&M University a collection of models of Chinese river junks made before World War II. Although the press's book* Junks of Central China, *by Professor Spencer, published in 1976, was a departure from the usual fare, it forecast an interest in nautical subjects that has continued to the present. Photograph by Jim Bones*

The years 1976 and 1977 were good ones for TAMUP. The press was accepted as a member of the Association of American University Presses. Very soon after the two-year waiting period required of new members, Wardlaw formally applied for membership on October 6, 1976, explaining that TAMUP had begun business on September 1, 1974. In his application he described the staff and their functions, as well as his efforts to keep overhead costs low by using freelance editors and contracting out computer operations. He reviewed the press's funding, including the character of the revolving funds. Wardlaw was proud of the fact that, even without a backlist, the new press had grossed $340,900 in sales in 1975–76. Texas A&M Press, he stressed, would emphasize the publication of books about Texas and the Southwest—books in art, history, and natural history, as well as any other fields focusing on this region. It would not publish fiction, poetry, juvenile literature, *Festschriften* (memorial volumes with contributions by several authors), or books by or about living politicians. It would concentrate on publishing outstanding contributions to knowledge in many fields of scholarship, but especially in areas in which the university was especially strong. Thus books dealing with the environment—air, energy, water, and land, as depicted by the press logo—would be emphasized.[30]

The books published in 1977 included: a volume about steam navigation on the Brazos River, an illustrated book in the Joe and Betty Moore Texas Art Series on old ranches of the Texas Plains, a collection of essays on the West by historian W. Eugene Hollon, an illustrated text on Fort Davis and the Texas frontier, and a biography of a nineteenth-century Texas immigrant from Germany. Walter Rundell's *Early Texas Oil: A Photographic History, 1866–1936,* the first volume in the Kenneth E. Montague Series in Oil History (which later was expanded to include business history), was published in 1977, as was Vandiver's *Black Jack: The Life and Times of John J. Pershing.* There were also books about the life of a working cowboy, bovine brucellosis, and the Japanese attack on Pearl Harbor.

"I have never worked harder or enjoyed it more," Wardlaw wrote to a friend in County Cork, Ireland. "In three or four years I will be retiring—and plan to find a place by the ocean in South Carolina."[31] Wardlaw's recurring illnesses hastened his planning both for retirement and for the press. In June, 1977, he wrote to Lloyd G. Lyman, executive editor and sales and promotion manager at Louisiana State University Press in Baton Rouge, "I called Les Phillabaum (director of the LSU Press) this morning and told him that I had designs on you. He said he would do everything he could to keep you, which doesn't surprise me." Wardlaw continued candidly, "Those in authority here know that you would be brought in with every expectation that you would become director when I retire. If you accept the associate directorship you will almost certainly succeed me as director unless you pull some

FIG. 14. Early Texas Oil: A Photographic History, 1866–1936, *by Walter Rundell, Jr., became the flagship volume in the Kenneth E. Montague Petroleum History Series in 1977. The series went on to include volumes on the early history of the oil industry in Oklahoma, Louisiana and Arkansas, and California, and in 1990 it was expanded to become the Kenneth E. Montague Series in Oil and Business History. This detail of a panorama by Charles Stark shows the Burkburnett Oil Field in 1919. Courtesy Harry Ransom Humanities Research Center, University of Texas at Austin*

colossal boner." At the time, five other university presses were looking for new directors, and Lyman was on all their lists. Meanwhile, the LSU Press was basking in the spectacular reception accorded John Kennedy Toole's *A Confederacy of Dunces*, an amazing book that would become a Pulitzer Prize–winning novel and a national bestseller. Wardlaw urged A&M's administration to move quickly on Lyman's appointment.[32]

Wardlaw and Lyman had chatted the previous year during the national meeting of the Association of American University Presses, held at Yale University. At that time, Wardlaw had asked Lyman to apply for the post of assistant director at TAMUP. Lyman, who had been at the University of California Press for sixteen years before going to LSU, was being championed for this position by August Frugé, longtime director of the University of California Press and a friend and associate of both Lyman and Wardlaw. Lloyd and Lea Lyman visited the A&M campus in the fall of 1976 and met with the press staff and President Williams. One of the things that struck Lyman on this first visit was the "extreme formality" of the A&M faculty. He recalled that each professor was addressed as Dr., while at California and LSU the salutation was Mr., Miss, or Mrs. He was also impressed, at the time as well as later, by Wardlaw's wide web of acquaintances. "He knew more people than most politicians." In any event, the job at Texas A&M was an intriguing opportunity. Nor was Wardlaw a person to whom it was easy to say no. Lyman accepted the job and began work on September 1, 1977.[33]

Lyman's entry into the world of scholarly book publishing, like that of most press directors, had been circuitous. In a world where relatively few university presses existed and where those that did exist generally enjoyed an uncertain status, one did not aspire to become a university press director. Where Lyman was born and raised, the only contact with scholarly publishing was this: some of the timber being harvested around Medford, Oregon, in the 1920s ended up in a pulp mill.

Lyman's father was a logging superintendent for the California Fruit Growers Exchange, which had substantial timber interests in northern California. The young man became associated with books and publishing in 1940, when he began undergraduate studies in history at Reed College, a small but prominent liberal arts college in Portland, Oregon. That initial association was brief. He joined the U.S. Navy in 1943 and, for the duration of the war, served in the Pacific aboard a transport ship, the USS *Todd.* When the war ended, Lyman's task force at Subic Bay in the Philippines was training for an invasion of Japan. He remembers sailing into Tokyo Bay past the battleship *Missouri* where the surrender was being signed. He spent the next year with American occupation forces in Japan, primarily ferrying Nationalist Chinese troops to northern China to combat the forces of Mao Tse-tung.[34]

Lyman returned to Reed College in 1946, finished his undergraduate degree in 1948, and enrolled in graduate studies in history at the University of California at Berkeley. In the process, he decided that he really did not want to teach, so he added a master's degree in library science to his master's in history. He then went to the California Institute of Technology, in Pasadena, as assistant librarian and instructor in history. There he was introduced to the director of the University of California Press, August Frugé, who convinced him that there was a life and a career in university publishing.

FIG. 15. *Lloyd Lyman succeeded Frank Wardlaw as director in September 1978 and continued in that position for ten years. He is shown here visiting the Hill Country retreat Friday Mountain, a camp established by historian Walter Prescott Webb to encourage historic preservation and the conservation of natural and human resources.*

In 1957, Lyman joined the University of California Press as assistant director. He directed and coordinated the press's production, marketing, business office, rights and permissions office, and personnel—and served as senior acquisitions editor.[35]

The sixteen years that Lyman worked in California were particularly good years for university presses. A large number of the university presses existing today were established during this period. According to the Association of American University Presses, these include: Pennsylvania State University Press (1956), Southern Illinois University Press (1956), Ohio State University Press (1957), Wesleyan University Press (1957), University of Arizona Press (1959), Massachusetts Institute of Technology Press (1961), University of Nevada Press (1961), University of Virginia Press (1963), Georgetown University Press (1964), University of Massachusetts Press (1964), Ohio University Press (1964), Kent State University Press (1965), University of Alberta (Canada) Press (1969), University of Iowa Press (1969), McGill University Press (1969), Temple University Press (1969), University of Mississippi Press (1970), University of New England Press (1970), and Texas Tech University Press (1971).

The Cold War, and most prominently the crisis of the American mind and spirit engendered by the launching of the first orbital satellite in October, 1957, had much to do with the expansion of university press publishing. That satellite, Sputnik I, was launched by the Soviet Union. Sen. Lyndon Baines Johnson said that "when news of Sputnik flashed across the globe . . . a new era of history dawned over the world." The United States, seemingly having lost its leadership in science and technology, felt threatened. The National Science Foundation submitted a special report to President Dwight D. Eisenhower indicating that, in the United States, basic research was seriously underemphasized. American students needed more and better science, math, physics, technical studies, and human medicine. Sen. Richard Nixon (among others) believed that Soviet scientific achievements underscored the need for racial integration in the public schools and expanded educational opportunities for all Americans.[36]

Congressional response to Sputnik was twofold. First, Congress approved the National Aeronautics and Space Administration Act of 1958, creating NASA and a far-reaching program of scientific and technical research that resulted in an accelerating demand for engineers, physicists, mathematicians, and technical people. Second, the National Defense Education Act of 1958 for the first time provided massive federal aid for public and higher education. In 1965, Congress followed with the Elementary and Secondary Education Act and, in 1966, created the National Endowment for the Humanities. Enrollment in educational institutions mushroomed. More research meant more journals and books needed to be published, and libraries were enlarged to accommodate the scholars and the new literature.

Almost unnoticed, the heightened academic activity gave rise to new university presses and an expansion of book publishing. Private foundations—the Ford Foundation in particular—gave lavishly to publishing projects. Quite simply, as Lyman observed, federal funding for education, stimulated earlier by the GI Bill and now the Cold War, space, civil rights, and science, meant that libraries and individuals had more money to spend for books and that new books were sought more eagerly.[37] These were, overall, good times for university presses. The "bad times" noted by Wardlaw, attendant upon the oil embargo and economic crisis of the early 1970s, were followed after 1977 by an era of exceptional growth in scholarly book publishing.

During his first year at Texas A&M, Lyman was in what he called "a learning mode." The new press proved to be quite different from the University of California Press, which had nearly one hundred employees and an annual list that sometimes exceeded one hundred titles. While the LSU Press experience had given Lyman some experience at a small press, the bookmaking world he encountered in College Station was unique. His main concern during that first year was becoming acquainted with Wardlaw's friends and associates, as well as with A&M's administrators and former students.[38] Lyman proved an eager student.

Plagued by recurring health problems and satisfied that the future of TAMUP would be in good hands, Wardlaw decided to move his retirement forward to September, 1978. He realized, however, that the press needed a firmer anchor to secure it in turbulent times. University administrations sometimes change rapidly, and subordinate units can be tossed about and aside amid ensuing changes. After suffering a heart attack in 1976, President Williams the following year had been promoted to the position of chancellor of the Texas A&M University System, and the press's director now reported to the chancellor's office. In August, 1977, Dr. Jarvis E. Miller, director of the Texas Agricultural Experiment Station and an Aggie (Class of 1950), became president of Texas A&M University. More changes seemed imminent.

A few months before his planned retirement, Wardlaw wrote to Williams, "As the day of my retirement draws near I want to suggest a plan which I believe will strengthen the Texas A&M University Press in the years that lie ahead." He remarked again upon the loyalty and devotion of Texas

Aggies to their school and the tremendous support the press had received from former students, who "individually and through their unusually effective association, have supported it in ways unique among universities with which I am acquainted." Wardlaw wanted to institutionalize that support by creating an advisory council for the press that would consist primarily of former students "plus a few other Texans of importance in the world of books."[39]

The press's Advisory Council (similar to organizations that existed at the University of California Press and Harvard University Press) would meet annually to receive a status report and to offer advice and guidance. Wardlaw asked that the council be created under the authority of the Board of Regents, with ten of its members to be nominated by the president of the Association of Former Students and five by the chancellor of the University System. The initial appointments would be for two years, with subsequent appointments staggered in order to permit continuity of service while making room for new members. "Perhaps you would be interested in the kind of people I have in mind for service on this council? They include men and women who have been especially helpful to the Press or who have exhibited unusual interest in the program." The individuals Wardlaw suggested represented a fascinating array of Aggies, artists, authors, businessmen, historians, ranchers, and Texans, suggesting the very wide web that Wardlaw had constructed in building patrons and support for the press. Copies of Wardlaw's letter to Williams were sent to Harvey Cash, president of the Association of Former Students, as well as to Buck Weirus, the association's executive director.[40]

Cash, Weirus, Williams, and the Board of Regents all agreed there was a need for an Advisory Council. Under Cash's oversight, Lyman, Weirus, and Wardlaw refined the list of alumni to be nominated by Cash, to include John H. Lindsey (Houston), Kenneth Montague (Houston), Joe Hiram Moore (Austin), John Caple (Fort Worth), J. Harold Dunn (Amarillo), Sterling C. Evans (San Antonio), H. C. Heldenfels (Corpus Christi), Edward J. Mosher (Houston), John R. Hill, Jr. (Dallas), and Ford D. Albritton, Jr. (Bryan). Wardlaw suggested that other nominees to be proposed by the chancellor might include Mrs. Maurice McAshan (Houston), Frank E. Vandiver (Houston), Carl C. Krueger, Jr. (Rockport), Mrs. Florence Rosengren (San Antonio), and Mrs. Chan Driscoll (Midland). When Williams saw the list he commented, "It will be a fantastic board."[41]

The list went through further refinements before final approval by the Board of Regents. Betty Moore, for example, took a seat on the Advisory Council in place of her husband, Joe. The regents also added A&M President Jarvis E. Miller, Prairie View A&M President Alvin A. Thomas, and Tarleton State University President William Trogdon. Comprising fifteen "strong friends of the press," the new council would meet annually in its capacity as a general advisory body.[42]

With the Advisory Council established, a good book list in production, and a strong and cooperative staff in place, Wardlaw retired on September 1, 1978. An outpouring of congratulations and good wishes from throughout the United States congratulated Wardlaw on a job well done. He was hailed repeatedly as a "living legend." Robert Barnes, director of Columbia University Press, described him as "The Legendary Frank Wardlaw: Three Times the Founder of a Press"—a title which, he said, reflected only a part of the legend. Among other titles offered were Wardlaw the Raconteur Supreme, Organizer of the Mexican Hegira, Pedernales River Guide, Friend, and Almost Worthy Husband of Rosemary.[43]

Francis E. Abernethy, historian and Texas folklorist, refrained from giving Wardlaw his "you-can't-go-home-again lecture" and commended him for having "brought a fine and finished quality to publishing that has had and will continue to have a lasting effect on Texas' literary image."[44]

Naturalist photographer Jim Bones wrote from the field, while photographing wildflowers:

> *As I waited for the wind to calm, my mind wandered with the melting snow down the Sangre de Cristo Mountains and out to the great river, across the bright expanse of New Mexico and West Texas into the green Lower Rio Grande Valley. I thought of Mr. Dobie's brush country in full bloom and of Paisano. And I thought of you, Frank.*[45]

Gayla Christiansen thought of how the press's first director had made each member of his staff "feel we were important to you and to A&M's Press and how you supported us, even when we stubbed our toes."[46]

Raconteur John Henry Faulk thought Wardlaw's leaving for Fripp Island was "glad-sad" news. "I feel it's something of an end of an era."

Llerena Friend, recently retired from the University of Texas archives, acknowledged him as "a moving force in the Texas literary and library world and all the time lighting up my life."

George Fuermann exclaimed, "Incomparably, you have been a man for all our seasons, one who has given me and God knows how many others the inside glow that precisely defines a word both warmhearted and bittersweet: friend!"

Houston columnist Leon Hale said, "Well, shoot, Frank. Just about the time we start getting well acquainted, you load up and leave. If you have to go, take along with you my personal gratitude for all you've done for those of us in Texas who try to make a living writing sentences."[47]

Frank Vandiver wrote, "You have, for more than three decades, enriched the intellectual life of the South, the Southwest, and the nation. In the years you've been in Texas you transformed Texans' appreciation of themselves and their region and you've elevated regionalism to the level of highest art."[48]

When Noel Parsons saw the small mountain of mail coming to Wardlaw upon his sixty-fifth birthday and retirement, he was amazed and then awestruck: "Your many friends appear to be gathered at random from among the rough and the polished, the learned and the less literate, the distinguished and the not-so-distinguished. Yet they all obviously have in common their love and admiration for you."[49] Parsons's words suggest the breadth of responses to Wardlaw's character, resolve, faith, dedication, and compassion.

Lyman, who became the Texas A&M University Press's second director on September 1, 1978, commented that, while the letters Wardlaw had received on the occasion of his retirement rehashed the past, he thought it also would be appropriate for him to "anticipate things to come."[50] Together with Christiansen, he orchestrated the retirement celebrations, writing hundreds of letters to friends of Wardlaw and of the A&M Press inviting their formal contributions to a letter book on the occasion of Wardlaw's sixty-fifth birthday and his impending retirement. Lyman instinctively knew (Wardlaw undoubtedly shared this view) that to commemorate Wardlaw in fact would be to commemorate the four-year-old Texas A&M University Press, elevate its status, and give it a new sense of permanence in the galaxy of university presses. Well before September 1, Lyman, with his predecessor's blessings and assistance, actually had assumed control of the press's affairs.

Not surprisingly, the fall book list came out on schedule. *Bataan and Beyond: Memories of an American POW*, by John S. Coleman, Jr., reaffirmed the role Texas Aggies had played in World War II. The book recalled the experiences of Maj. Gen. George Moore (a former commandant of the Corps of Cadets and a 1908 A&M graduate) and of other Aggies who were taken prisoner by the Japanese at Bataan and Corregidor in the early months of World War II.

A third volume in the Joe and Betty Moore Art Series, *Buck Schiwetz' Memories,* was composed of a half-century's paintings and drawings, with a text by columnist Leon Hale. The 1978 fall list also included books on Polish Americans and on western fiction, a collection of economics essays entitled *Liberty and the Rule of Law,* and a pioneering study of cottonseed oil production and agricultural cooperatives by William N. Stokes, Jr.

The transition was remarkably smooth, considering that Lyman followed in the footsteps of a legend. Lyman was a man with great "people" skills, great energy, and a strong determination sometimes obscured by his easygoing affability. He delegated, consulted, and sought the frequent counsel of his staff. Lyman worked arduously and circumspectly at retaining the associations, impetus, and directions developed by Wardlaw during the first four years of the press's operation. He maintained close contact by letter and in person with A&M administrators and such press patrons as Joe and Betty Moore, John Lindsey, Kenneth Montague, and Jack Williams. He understood that Williams had been critical both to the creation of the press and, now, to its continuing survival.

In October, Lyman laid plans for assembling the Advisory Council that Wardlaw had worked so diligently to create before his retirement. He asked Chancellor Williams to extend invitations for a council meeting prior to the Texas Christian University football game on November 25, 1978. The meeting was scheduled for the director's office in the old Board of Directors Building, to be followed by lunch with Chancellor and Mrs. Williams, who had moved into the ground-floor apartment there after the Wardlaws left. Lyman, frugal by nature, was delighted that the chancellor would bear the cost of the luncheon, since the press's "contingency funds will have nearly disappeared."[51]

As it turned out, the Williamses held a coffee for the Advisory Council in their apartment, and President Miller invited the members to the president's pre-game luncheon at the Memorial Student Center. At the meeting, Wardlaw, in his new capacity as "consulting editor," presented a briefing on the status of the press and offered his farewells prior to leaving for retirement in South Carolina. The main business of the council was to elect a chairperson. Appropriately, the person chosen was Lindsey, who had just received the university's Distinguished Alumnus award and who had had so much to do with the press's founding.[52]

The Wardlaws found their retirement home on Fripp Island a not entirely safe refuge. A hurricane struck the island that first spring and was followed by exceptionally high tides in the fall, but the couple weathered the storms; recouped their losses; fished for bass, whiting, flounder, and shark from the deck over their revetment (stone shoring up the embankment); and remained in close contact by letter with their old friends in Texas.[53]

Meanwhile, the press's second director turned his attention primarily to acquisitions. Lyman became a frequenter of meetings for regional and national history, science, and literary studies. His primary interest at first was to maintain the list and the direction established by Wardlaw. But he also wanted to "grow the list." Wardlaw's initial goal of publishing twenty books a year while maintaining a small but quality operation would not suffice to carry TAMUP into national prominence or allow it to attain the stature of other university presses. Nor was a small publication list economically viable, especially during inflationary times. Lyman wanted to maintain the strong regional base of the press while extending its reach nationally. He wanted to broaden the list of publications to include "crossover" books—that is, titles capable of appealing to both scholarly and trade book markets.[54]

For all of its revolving fund accounts and financial support, the new press (like most university presses) continued to walk a fiscal tightrope. The revolving funds were good and essential, but publication of a book using resources from a fund meant that money had been borrowed from that fund. This money had to be repaid or replaced, or the fund would cease to exist. The press's administrative and operating expenses also had to be covered, in part, by the sale of books. A healthy cash flow was essential to continuing business. Simply put, in order to assure survival of the various series and of the press, books not only had to be quality products, but also had to sell. Lyman reasoned that the more books the press had in print, the greater the cash flow and the greater the chances for economic survival.[55] Thus TAMUP's direction was shaped not only by the definition of its series and publishing policy, but also by the practical realities of marketing and sales.

FIG. 16. *The Board of Directors Building burned on the morning of February 28, 1979. The press offices on the second floor were almost totally destroyed by flames, smoke, and water, and the home of Chancellor Jack Williams and his wife, on the first floor where the Wardlaws had previously lived, was irreparably water-damaged. The building was later demolished and the land was cleared for the construction of Hobby and Neeley Halls. Courtesy University Archives, Texas A&M University*

TAMUP's direction also was influenced by a combination of wholly unforeseen events. On January 23, 1979, Chancellor Jack K. Williams, who had been so instrumental in the press's creation, resigned. During the eight years of his administration, Texas A&M University had experienced the greatest growth in its history, with student enrollment doubling from fourteen thousand students in 1970 to more than thirty thousand in the fall of 1978. The physical campus likewise had expanded. Funding had increased, especially in the areas of research and graduate program development. And the new Texas A&M University Press had come into being. While the year of its creation might have been, in the national context, the worst possible time to organize a university press, in the context of Texas A&M University's history the timing had been favorable. Even so, the press could not have been established, Lyman believed, without the strong support of President Williams.[56] Now the fledgling press found itself adrift amid administrative change, and its logo—air, earth, fire, and water—soon would acquire new resonance.

The year 1979 began with considerable promise. The Board of Regents authorized the badly needed reconstruction and remodeling of the Texas A&M University Press (Old Board of Directors) Building, which had been built in 1912. With that work under way, the press continued to operate amid electricians, painters, carpenters, and a continuing flow of visitors, faculty, and authors. Then an unforeseen event occurred.

On Tuesday, February 28, fire engulfed the press building, consuming the roof and a large portion of the top floor before firemen could extinguish the flames. The building was a total loss, but fortunately no one, including

FIG. 17. *This Texas A&M University Centennial commemorative pewter plate hung on the wall of Lloyd Lyman's office at the time of the fire, and part of it was melted away. Manuscript, proof, and other documents on the conference table in Lyman's office were protected by a large ceiling lamp fixture that fell and covered them.*

Frank

Your friendship has held a special place in my heart ever since that summer evening back in 1950 when we met in Frank Dobie's back yard. I am proud to think that you have allowed me to be a kind of an associate of yours – through the designing of your two press marks – in the superb work you have done throughout all the years of your matchless accomplishment in Texas. You have given all of us so much! May your ease now be all happy; may you carry with you always our admiration, our gratitude and our love.

Tom Lea

FIG. 18. *The results of the fire are demonstrated by this copy of a letter written by Tom Lea to Frank Wardlaw on the occasion of Wardlaw's retirement. Lea illustrated the letter with a combination of his designs for the pressmarks of Texas A&M University Press and the University of Texas Press, both of which Wardlaw had initiated. The press staff had the job of salvaging thousands of similar charred, water-soaked sheets.*

the Williams family, still in residence, was injured. Students from nearby dormitories rushed to the scene and boldly rushed into the flaming building to help retrieve personal effects from the chancellor's home—even to the point of carrying out the Williamses' piano. The press offices were spared some destruction because the inner ceiling of the building collapsed on filing cabinets, tables, and desks and thus helped protect manuscripts and financial records from fire and water damage. Most of the manuscripts already accepted for publication were either out of the building or were saved through an "act of Providence."[57]

John A. Adams, Jr., recalled rushing to the scene to find his manuscript on the history of the Former Students Association (which had just been approved for publication) sitting intact on Lloyd Lyman's desk with only minor scorching and water damage. Valuable paintings (including those by Buck Schiwetz) and many irreplaceable photographs had been stored safely in vaults outside the building. But there were losses. Lyman described other materials in the offices as "charred goo." The press's quarters, then in the final stages of renovation, were gone. Curiously, the only manuscripts lost in the fire were ones the press already had decided to reject. Trying to salvage a bit of humor from the trying situation, Lyman joked, "I can just hear some poor author right now saying to somebody, 'Rejection is one thing, but did they have to burn my manuscript?' "[58]

The shipping room, a concrete-block annex (originally a garage) that housed most of the books in stock, escaped damage. The staff moved into the shipping room while workmen cleared the debris from the site, and the Advisory Council, regents, and university administrators pondered what to do next. The elements of the TAMUP logo—air, earth, fire, and water—had taken on a tangible dimension.

Chapter 3

UP FROM THE ASHES

"Bad news travels fast," Lyman wrote within the week to members of TAMUP's Advisory Council, "so you may have already heard the worst news about the Press since its establishment five years ago." The press was homeless, its building burned. "Just where we will find new quarters, even on a temporary basis, has not yet been determined."[1]

For the new director, these were tough times in more ways than one. The university's administration was undergoing major changes. Jack K. Williams, TAMUP's founder, invaluable partisan, and friend (as well as the man to whom the press director reported), had tendered his resignation as chancellor on January 23, 1979, with the brief announcement: "This will be my last board meeting. I am resigning as chancellor, effective today." The Board of Regents then named its chairman, Clyde H. Wells, acting chancellor and began the search for Williams's replacement.[2]

With literally no place to go and nothing else to do, the press resumed operations—in the garage: "Not a day was lost in order fulfillment, and the business of the Press has progressed uninterrupted, although the entire staff and all remaining equipment and files are now crowded into the former Directors' garage, which has been converted into a shipping room. It is a splendid tribute to the quality of the staff that they are able to carry on so efficiently under these circumstances." Lloyd Lyman continued in his situation report to Chancellor Wells, "However, temporary quarters (including among other things bathroom facilities) are urgently needed."[3]

Don Collins had been in Chicago on the night of the fire and received a call from Gayla Christiansen the next morning. He flew back to College Station on the first available flight. As soon as the embers cooled, the entire staff (including Bill Shearer, an A&M graduate who only recently had joined the Press staff as sales representative) began the cleanup, making endless trips up and down the soggy, ash-covered stairs and dodging the sagging ceiling to carry out wet but usable furniture and soaked papers. Salvaged desks, chairs, and cabinets were transported to the nearby garage and shipping room. Papers and manuscripts were spread out on the parking lot to dry. Parsons particularly remembers Jerry Cooper, editor of the *Texas Aggie,* coming to lend a hand and spending many hours of his own time in the cleanup.[4] Through these efforts, the staff was able to save much that otherwise might have been lost.

The next problem, Collins recalled, was figuring out what to do with the files and records that had been salvaged. The solution was to move the books to one side of the eight-car garage that served as a shipping and storage area. For a few weeks, shipping went on in one half of the garage, while the business of publishing went on in the other half.[5] It was not an easy life.

Two weeks following the fire, Lyman, John Lindsey, chair of the Advisory Council; Haskell Monroe, chair of the Faculty Advisory Committee; and Ford Albritton, Advisory Council member, met with Chancellor Wells to discuss the future of TAMUP. They decided that the best course would be for the press to resume operations temporarily in mobile units that could be installed near the shipping room, while the administration and regents studied several options: salvaging the Old Board of Directors Building, relocating the press, or building a new building for TAMUP using money received from the state's self-insurance program to help cover construction costs. Another possibility raised but rejected was to move the press's operations to the basement of the Reed McDonald Building on campus. (This structure also housed the university printing center. In the past the latter had, for a time, been known as the A&M Press.) Collins suggested moving into the historic Hirshfeld House in Austin, which had just been donated to Texas A&M University by Joe and Betty Moore. This idea was quickly rejected because TAMUP had, in fact, become "an integral part of the University" and must remain on campus.[6]

When the Board of Regents met on March 26 to consider what should

FIG. 19. *John H. Lindsey, the first person to support Texas A&M University having a press, has consistently been a longtime supporter of the press.*

be done, opinions were mixed. President Miller proposed that the burned structure be razed and a dormitory be built in its place—with press offices to be constructed somewhere else at a future time. Miller and Chancellor Wells recommended that the press be temporarily housed in portable buildings estimated to cost about $50,000. Some regents objected to placing mobile homes on the campus, even on a temporary basis, while others countered that such facilities already existed on campus at various construction sites.[7]

Meanwhile, working conditions were posing a severe trial to staff morale and efficiency. The crowded, makeshift garage offices became stifling as the weather grew warmer. In June, the university located three mobile office units for the press staff's use. Lyman noted that, while accommodations remained "spartan," working conditions were so much improved "that we cannot complain."[8]

In July, the special committee appointed by the Board of Regents to study the possibility of restoring the Old Board of Directors Building voted to demolish the building and to construct a dormitory on the site. Lindsey, the only committee member supporting restoration, confessed to the Advisory Council that he had "no idea where the Press will be located or when permanent quarters will be approved."[9]

Despite improvements, working conditions continued to pose hardships. Nor did it help matters when, in early August, Lyman was informed that the temporary press quarters could no longer be located near the Old Board of Directors Building, because construction of the proposed women's dormitory had to proceed. Frank Vandiver, provost and vice president of Rice University and a member of the Advisory Council, wrote to Lindsey and others in August that he sensed a "growing morale problem at the Press . . . stoked by the feeling that the Press is apparently underappreciated at the University." Vandiver affirmed that the "Press is, as you know, a real adornment to the academic scene at A&M, and I think it's simply too fine an asset to let wither and decline." Lindsey, Sterling C. Evans, and other members of the Advisory Council in turn wrote to Chancellor Wells expressing their concern. On August 20, perhaps partly in response to these inquiries, Wells reported to Lindsey that the Regents had decided not to attempt to restore the "Old Board House" and would raze the building "this week."[10] But no decision was made on where or how to house TAMUP permanently.

On September 27, 1979, the Board of Regents appointed a new chancellor for the Texas A&M University System, Frank W. R. Hubert, dean of the College of Education. That same month, the university administration proposed a new Texas A&M University Press building, contingent upon approval of funding by the state legislature. The legislature did not approve the funding.[11]

Even so, the university began an earnest assessment and study for a new TAMUP building. Lyman obtained plans and specifications for comparable university press facilities, made an analysis, and drafted a report projecting

FIG. 20. *Frank E. Vandiver, president of Texas A&M University from 1981 to 1988, established a relationship with the press as early as 1977 with publication of his first book,* Black Jack: The Life and Times of John J. Pershing. *Since then the press has published or reissued five other books and an audiotape by Vandiver.*

TAMUP's needs. In November, 1979, he submitted a calculation that the press would require some nineteen thousand–plus square feet of operating space, including storage, for the next five to ten years.[12]

In the spring of 1980, business manager Don Collins cautioned that the press's off-campus warehouse (which contained approximately 3,200 square feet and was located at the Riverside Annex, nearly seven miles from the main campus) was reaching capacity. Some seventy-eight thousand books were in storage. While insulation and ventilation had been installed to control humidity, the building was a wood-frame structure and hence was

FIG. 21. *Frank W. R. Hubert, chancellor of the Texas A&M University System, 1979–82, was the main proponent for a new building for the press. He presented the idea to the Board of Regents, which approved the building in 1981.*

vulnerable to fire damage. Moreover, the annex had no foam truck for fighting fires, and pouring water on the books probably would damage them as much as a fire would. Another storage space located on campus, encompassing 1,800 square feet, was even less secure than the annex. Collins estimated that, within the year, the press would require two thousand square feet of additional storage space. For the next five to ten years, a minimum of fifteen thousand more square feet of humidity-controlled, secure storage would be needed.[13] Lyman's preliminary estimates of a total of about twenty thousand square feet for new facilities already were inadequate.

Space requirements soon would expand even more dramatically. Amid the difficulties caused by the fire, TAMUP made a remarkable breakthrough in sales and distribution—although, Collins said, at the time he was unaware of the full significance of the new developments.

Don Collins, a native of Stephenville, Texas, was a business graduate of Tarleton State College, which made him "almost" an Aggie. After graduation, he accepted a job with General Dynamics in Fort Worth, but he found the work very stressful because of the "boom-or-bust" business cycle characteristic of the aerospace industry, with its attendant job insecurity. By chance he encountered Dohn Barham, an old friend from Stephenville who was business manager of the University of Texas Press. Barham asked Collins if he would accept a job working for him as assistant business manager at UTP. Collins was intrigued but noncommittal. When interviewed by Frank Wardlaw, Collins discovered that "you simply cannot tell Wardlaw no." He joined the Wardlaw team in Austin.[14]

When the Texas A&M Press began releasing its publications, Wardlaw asked Collins to come talk to him about becoming business manager at the new press. Collins agreed to come for a visit, expecting to tell Wardlaw that he would not accept the job at A&M. But when he arrived, Collins found himself seated across the table from both Wardlaw and Jack Williams, in what became a two-hour interview. The two cast a spell. It was a great feeling, Collins recalled, to know that the president of the university truly believed in the press's work.[15]

Collins began work as business manager on July 1, 1975. He sold and packed books, helped entertain, met visitors at the airport, and, like others on the staff, did whatever needed doing. It was a family situation—everyone pitched in, did his or her share, and helped the head of the family, who happened to be Frank Wardlaw. Collins's first job was to go on the road selling TAMUP books to bookstores. He usually spent four days on the road, returned on Fridays, and used the weekends to prepare preliminary invoices and pack books for shipment. The preliminary invoices went to the University of Texas Press for final printing and mailing. While Collins sold and packed, Grimaila and Wardlaw handled catalog preparation and mail orders. When Bill Shearer joined the press staff, he assumed the duties of sales representative. Shearer's road trips helped build a strong sales base for the fledgling press, creating new pressures on storage, shipping, and order processing.[16]

In 1976, the press asked the university's new data processing center, referred to as Computing Services, to prepare software, so the press could process its own orders and invoices. Gradually it became apparent that the mainframe computer systems were not suitable for the kinds of operations the press required. Working with Collins, Christiansen, and Lyman, Don Beaugez helped develop software so that TAMUP could handle its own shipments using personal computers. By 1977, a system had been set up that allowed the press to allocate its sales and income among its various revolving accounts. Collins explained, "We had to keep our dollars separated for each account."[17]

That requirement became a critical component in TAMUP's becoming a marketing and distribution facility for other university presses. In 1982 Rice approached Lyman about a possible distribution arrangement. Also in that year, Keith Gregory, then director of Texas Christian University Press, asked Collins to come to Fort Worth as a consultant to help him solve some marketing and accounting problems. In the course of their discussion, Collins commented to Gregory that, since TAMUP had solved its distribution and billing problems, it would make good sense for the TCU Press to let A&M handle its shipping, warehousing, and sales, while the staff in Fort Worth concentrated on procurement and book production.[18] This proved a happy solution to a difficult problem, not just for TCU but also for several other university presses in Texas.

Lyman, Christiansen, and Collins discussed the distribution idea with the staff of the Rice University Press and Rice's Provost Frank E. Vandiver. In January, 1983, Rice University Press entered into a distribution agreement with Texas A&M University Press, by which TAMUP agreed to provide warehousing, shipping, billing, collecting, and accounting services in return for a percentage of Rice's gross sales. TCU Press signed a similar agreement in May, 1983. During 1983 and 1984, the press entered into an additional distribution agreement with the Texas State Historical Association and took on handling books for the John E. Conner Museum at Texas A&I University in Kingsville, the Texas Forest Service, and the Texas Agricultural Extension Service. Southern Methodist University Press and the University of North Texas Press had joined the consortium by the end of the decade.[19]

In the early 1980s, when these distribution arrangements were just beginning, the Texas A&M Press published about thirty books per year and generated over $600,000 in total annual revenues. In later years, Don Collins integrated aspects of TAMUP's distribution system into the operations of the University of Chicago Press, where he serves as chief financial officer.[20]

During the early 1980s, the press staff made intensive studies of space and equipment needs, while attempting to conduct business as usual. Slowly, however, certain realities became clear. Not only had the fire irrevocably altered TAMUP operations, but also, in the decades after 1970, book publishing as a whole was being transformed by changes in distribution and in the technology of book production. The world of manual typewriters, lead type, small presses, and the Wardlaw style of publishing was passing away.

To be sure, under any technology the business of book publishing was a time-consuming, complex, and sometimes convoluted business. Authors continued to begin the process with an idea and convert ideas into words—on three, four, five, or six hundred pages of paper, and most often in two, three, or four drafts. The process could take years. At the close of the 1970s, most authors still were pounding out their manuscripts on manual typewriters and using carbon copies. The more technologically sophisticated used electric typewriters, some of them with "lift-off correction tape" for making corrections without erasures or manually whiting out errors. Computers and xerographic copiers were waiting in the wings, but writing a book took time. So did publishing one.

Traditionally, an author wrote a letter of inquiry, sometimes accompanied by sample chapters, asking if a press would be interested in publishing her or his manuscript. Sometimes that inquiry came in response to a request or solicitation by a press's acquisitions staff, or through a press's being recommended by a published author or a friend of the press. Sometimes a press initiated a project by inviting a prospective author to write a particular book.

Once a manuscript was in hand, the director, editor, and other staff members considered the manuscript before deciding if it merited further review. The review process intended by Wardlaw in 1976 provided that a manuscript should be reviewed for publication by a three-person committee chosen from the Faculty Advisory Committee or from the general faculty at Texas A&M, depending on the special knowledge required. A fourth member of the manuscript review committee was selected from the Faculty Advisory Committee to serve as a nonspecialist "honest broker" reviewer. Although initially the fate of publication rested upon the four-person committee, soon the practice developed of having manuscripts reviewed by specialists (whether inside or outside the A&M University community), with the reports then being submitted to a select committee of the Faculty Advisory Committee for final approval or disapproval.[21]

Occasionally, final review resulted in the rejection of a book proposed for publication, and sometimes the review required further revisions by an author, but most often the Advisory Committee agreed to publish the book under the TAMUP imprint. All of this meant that months—sometimes a year or more—might pass before the press accepted a manuscript for publication. At that point the "in press" process began.

Authors first were charged to revise or correct a manuscript in line with criticisms raised by reviewers. The revised manuscript (whenever it appeared) then was turned over to an editor for copyediting. The copyeditor applied careful language, grammar, and stylistic criteria to the manuscript to make it a correct, clear, and readable work. The copyedited manuscript then was returned to the author for review, acceptance, or alteration as required.

Upon its return, the copyedited manuscript went to the production department for design. The production manager submitted the manuscript to a professional typesetter for composition. Well into the 1980s, the first set of proofs was the galley proof, which contained all the words and sentences of the manuscript, but not yet in page format. After a review of the galley proof by the copyeditor and author, the galleys were returned to the typesetter for setting in page proof. In the days of hot lead, which began in the fifteenth century and drew to a close about the time TAMUP was founded, proof was set by hand by the typesetter; by the 1970s, however, most typesetters had converted to Linotype, an operation introduced in the 1880s, by which type was set on a manually operated keyboard. In the 1950s, phototypesetting processes began replacing Linotype operations. With the introduction and spread of desktop publishing (personal computer systems), typography and printing processes were further revolutionized.

By the mid-1980s, computers and improved word-processing software had begun streamlining the writing, editing, and composition processes to the extent that a book need never leave the electronic media before appearing in a bound and printed volume. The first twenty years of TAMUP's existence, then, witnessed a veritable revolution in processes of writing, printing, and publishing.

The new technology did not necessarily mean that a given book would be released (published or printed) in a shorter time (the traditional two or three years, including review and revision times, remained typical), but that more manuscripts could flow through the process, producing a larger annual list of books with the same staff and facilities. By 1980, Lyman and TAMUP had made a conscious decision to expand annual book production substantially. This increase required more careful and more detailed planning and scheduling for production—often years in advance.

At TAMUP and elsewhere, the decision to expand the publication list only in part was driven by the opportunities created by new and improved technology. To a greater extent, the expansion was dictated by simple financial realities. Larger book lists and larger inventories tended to yield more income and hence greater security for a press—whether university or commercial. Expanded production lists also meant new tensions between volume production and quality control. When more manuscripts were published, did the quality of the resulting books—in terms of content, editing, design, and composition—decline? If the quality did decline, did it at least remain acceptable by the high standards of university presses? With more titles being produced, did the increase in income offset the rise in costs? Issues of quality and quantity would continue to arise as book lists expanded.

From a different standpoint, TAMUP, beginning with its 1983 spring list, produced more books and tried to maximize efficiency in use of its existing resources. Mary Lenn Dixon (who joined the staff as an assistant editor in September, 1978) remembers the shift in publishing policy that began about 1979, when Lyman decided that the press needed to grow—although the products of that shift would not be visible for several years.[22]

Dixon's arrival at the press was an integral part of that growth. Her move into publishing, like that of many in the business, was somewhat accidental. Indeed, many refer to university press publishing as an "accidental profession." A native of Hamilton, a small community in Central Texas, Dixon graduated from the University of Texas with a combined major in government and English. She earned a Ph.D. in political science from the University of Wisconsin and, in 1974, accepted a job teaching in the political science department at Texas A&M. Dixon remembered receiving the first TAMUP catalog, announcing the publication of six books.[23]

In 1978, when Dixon decided to begin looking for other opportunities within the university system, she visited with Chancellor Jack Williams. Williams laughed and told her that there was one place on campus that he felt "had the most energy, the most creativity, and the best esprit de corps": the new university press. He advised her to investigate.[24] Several months passed. On impulse one day that summer, Dixon called the press offices and talked with Margaret Ingram, then managing editor. She described her qualifications and wondered if the press might be interested. Ingram replied that, by a strange coincidence, she had just walked out of a staff meeting in which a decision had been made to hire a new assistant editor. She encouraged Dixon to apply. Wardlaw, who already had announced his retirement, deferred the hiring decision to Lloyd Lyman, making Dixon Lyman's first "hire" as TAMUP director.[25]

Dixon described her joining TAMUP as "coming home to a home I never knew I had." Editing, Dixon said, is like working a puzzle. She liked the relative independence and anonymity of the work and also enjoyed the "nurturing" role of the editor.[26] An editor's job was to make an author out of a writer, and often that required enormous care, patience, and support.

Lyman's decision to "grow the press" meant that, while most copyediting continued to be done by the staff, some of that work now had to be contracted out to freelance editors. The role of the in-house editor increasingly became that of an intermediary who was an "author relations" specialist. By early 1981, the press had augmented its manuscript acquisitions. The work grew with the lists.[27]

Ingram, who headed the editorial staff, saw her responsibilities expand considerably, due to increased manuscript submissions, training the new editor, and supervising the development of commissioned books. She was responsible for acquisitions, development, and initial screening of manuscripts, "all of which require more time and concentrated effort than is now possible." She had to oversee copyeditors, freelance editors, and indexers, as well as completing her own copyediting assignments. Ingram suggested that more secretarial help be added, that each copyeditor for a book project have responsibility for supervising freelance editing, that editors be assigned series responsibilities, and that controls and review processes be standardized and improved.[28]

As the lists and the work began to grow, staff meetings grew more intense. Lyman delegated more of the decisions and responsibilities to the staff than Wardlaw had. That heightened the sense of professionalism. While being crowded together in the mobile office unit increased tension and stress, it also forced the staff into a strong camaraderie, creating an esprit de corps that otherwise might have been missing in the aftermath of the fire.[29]

Extensive lists of book ideas gleaned from author inquiries, correspondence, submitted manuscripts, and references were reviewed regularly at weekly staff meetings. The staff considered production schedules and the need for balance in the book lists, producing tentative spring and fall lists of titles scheduled for publication. If the production schedule proceeded as planned, by spring or fall the press had a firm list of books scheduled for publication for the subsequent season six months later—and produced a catalog announcing the scheduled publication.

For example, in February, 1980, the staff met in the mobile units' conference area and reviewed fifteen titles that potentially could be ready for publication in the spring of 1981. Of those fifteen titles, five were eliminated because reader reviews had not been completed, changes suggested by readers had not been completed by the authors, or money was not available for publication at that time. Among the titles cleared for the 1981 spring list was a book about nautical archaeology. *Yassi Ada,* volume 1: *A Seventh-Century Byzantine Shipwreck,* by George F. Bass and Frederick H. van Doorninck, Jr., reported an undersea exploration by Texas A&M University's nautical archaeology team. That team had come into being in 1976, when Texas A&M University invited George Bass and his three-year-old American Institute of Nautical Archaeology (later simply the Institute of Nautical Archaeology) to move to College Station. The institute had its Mediterranean headquarters on the Isle of Cyprus. Bass agreed and soon was joined by fellow archaeologist van Doorninck and by J. Richard Steffy, a skilled craftsman and modeler who had become one of the world's leading authorities on ancient shipbuilding and the interpretation of undersea archaeology. With publication funded in part by a subvention from the Institute of Nautical Archaeology, *Yassi Ada* became the first of several prestigious books in TAMUP's Nautical Archeology Series.[30]

Other titles tentatively approved for spring of 1981 included *H. W. Caylor, Frontier Artist;* a history of the southern railroad system by Keith L. Bryant, Jr.; a biography of Mexico's President Alvaro Obregón, entitled *Power and*

FIG. 22. *The Institute for Nautical Archaeology, under the direction of Dr. George F. Bass, moved to Texas A&M University not long before the press was established. In 1982 the press published the first in what has turned out to be a long and successful list in nautical archaeology.* Yassı Ada: Volume I, A Seventh-Century Byzantine Shipwreck, *edited by Bass, Frederick H. Van Doorninck, and others, set a high standard for the volumes that followed. Here, a diving-trained archaeologist surveys the site.*

Revolution in Mexico: The Rise of Alvaro Obregón, 1911–1920, by Linda Hall; a study of water controversies in Los Angeles, California; a book about electron valence theory by Anthony N. Stranges; a book on Oklahoma oil, published in the Montague Series in Oil and Business History; a cultural atlas; and an anthropological study, tentatively entitled *Wangka,* by Edwin Doran. At the same meeting, eighteen titles were placed on a tentative list for publication in fall of 1981.[31]

In addition to the constant assessment and review of books nearing publication, weekly or monthly the staff reviewed extensive lists of "revisions in the works" and "manuscripts under consideration—in-house." These lists ordinarily contained thirty or more titles at some stage of consideration. During the review process, the number of copies proposed for publication, the estimated cost of publishing each title, and the price at which the book was to be marketed were established. Sales and marketing staff—most prominently, Gayla Christiansen and Bill Shearer—evaluated book manuscripts from the real-life perspective of the marketplace. In theory, university publishing was not a profit-making enterprise, but neither the presses nor their universities could tolerate large deficits.[32]

In the five years following Frank Wardlaw's retirement, the fire, and Jack K. Williams's resignation as TAMU chancellor—years easily considered difficult and stressful—the A&M Press made giant strides. To be sure, this progress was not made without the assistance of the Advisory Council, the Faculty Advisory Committee, authors and friends of the press, and Texas A&M University administrators. Notable among the latter group was Chancellor Frank W. R. Hubert.

Hubert was extremely supportive of the press and sympathetic to its plight in the aftermath of the fire. It was he who mustered Board of Regents support for a new building. In fact, Lyman recalled that some months after the fire, a regent and a top university administrator had told him that "the likelihood of the A&M Press getting a new building was very slight." Indeed, said Lyman, at most campuses the university press tended to be housed in older, less desirable locations.[33]

In October, 1980, responding to concerns about the status, or lack of status, of the press and seeing a problem that needed fixing, Hubert initiated the preliminary studies and surveys required for construction of a new building, with the understanding that, if legislative funding were not approved for the project, the university would provide funds (estimated at $2,060,300) from the University Available Fund (the interest from the Permanent University Fund). During development of the building proposal, Jarvis Miller resigned as university president and was replaced by Interim President Charles H. Samson, Jr., longtime head of the department of civil engineering. Samson concurred in Hubert's decision to do something about Press facilities and signed off on the planning initiative, as did Gen. Wesley E. Peel, director of facilities planning and construction, and Howard Vestal, vice president for business affairs. The job of coordinating the planning was given to Robert S. Boyce, architect in the Facilities Planning Division.[34]

Documentation justifying the request for a new building included a letter from Sterling C. Evans, who forwarded comments from William N. Stokes, Jr., a former director of the Lubbock Oil Mill and a graduate of the University of Texas. Stokes described TAMUP as one of the two most prestigious college presses in this part of the nation:

> *A reputation such as this is something which requires continuing encouragement, nurturing and promotion. I am fearful that the current authorities may not realize, first the reputation which has been achieved, and secondly the importance of continuing to build and improve it. . . . The authorities should realize that the press is the window opening onto the whole intellectual world; if closed or darkened, it's a hurt to the institution; opportunities for expanding it are legion and should be pursued.*

The university's justification for building the press a new home included recognition that, "like the rest of Texas A&M, the Press's rate of growth has been unique. No other university press has come so far as quickly." Not only should the new building provide adequate space for the press's staff, but also it should have a "separate character of its own that distinguishes it from other university activities."[35]

The administration's unequivocal commitment to the new building soon was submitted to some severe tests. The university had decided to build the new building on the near-sacred grounds of Duncan Field, where Aggies traditionally held an annual bonfire before the University of Texas football game. Students thought the building's location was an exceptionally bad choice. Letters and articles in the student newspaper, *The Battalion,* voiced strong objections: the bonfire was an Aggie tradition and should continue to be held on Duncan Field. One member of the student senate introduced a "University Press Location Bill" condemning the proposed location. A *Battalion* cartoon suggested a compromise between those opposed to locating the TAMUP building on Duncan Field and the administration: "Starting next year, and annually thereafter, a university press building will be constructed out of logs on the present site, and then burned to the ground."[36]

The administration weathered the storm. Site preparation began on March 1, 1981. For the next two years, the director and staff were intensely involved in expanding the publication lists as well as in planning, purchasing, designing, revising, and monitoring construction of the new building—all within the confines of three corridor-linked mobile office units which soon were joined by an even more mobile separate unit used for conferences.

Unfortunately, the mobile conference room proved a little too mobile, since it "encroached" upon space used by residents of Hotard Hall, a men's dormitory, for ballgames and recreation. On several occasions when the staff returned to work in the morning, they found that the mobile conference room had been moved to another location in order to clear the field for play. Usually enough students from Hotard or another men's dormitory could be found to push the unit back into place. Eventually the conference room was anchored to the other work units. Nevertheless, upon occasion editors continued to be startled from their engrossed study of manuscripts by the impact of a wayward football or baseball hitting the sheet-metal walls of the mobile units. Press staff suspected that students sometimes actually took pleasure in banging on the wall or ceilings.[37] After all, the press was located on the playing field. Building the new building on the bonfire field might prove equally hazardous.

Publishing was hazardous in other ways. Growth entailed higher printing and production costs. Years might pass before sales revenues would cover the costs of publishing a book. TAMUP's operating capital was declining to dangerous levels. In March, 1981, Lyman wrote a lengthy letter to Chancellor Hubert explaining how inflation had cut sales revenues while raising expenses. Costs were rising and were going to rise even more, he said, as the press increased its number of publications "from fifteen to twenty titles per year to twenty to thirty titles per year." To accomplish its goals, the press would require substantially more funding. Moreover, given the inflation indexes, the decline in trade sales, and the fact that at least 25 percent of the operations budget was tied directly to income from sales, the press might "eventually be without capital to publish popular trade books and without a staff adequate to publish scholarly titles."[38]

In April, 1982, Chancellor Hubert asked Lyman to prepare a preliminary draft of a "minute order" requesting $200,000 from the University Available Fund for transfer to the TAMUP general operating account. In June, Hubert invited Lyman to present a briefing on the status of the press to the Board of Regents. At that meeting, Lyman described a university press as a "very personal venture" whose success depended not only upon the staff, the authors, and the buyers of books, but upon the governing board of its parent institution. In the past six years, Lyman said, the press had created a backlist of one hundred titles, distributed 230,000 books, and generated a total sales income of $2.4 million—all during times of general financial distress and under the physical adversities and difficult working conditions resulting from the fire. Lyman extolled the success of the various series and commented on particularly successful titles. "The publications of the first six years of the Press are an unprecedented accomplishment," he said, "unmatched by any other university press in a comparable time period. But this is only a beginning!"[39]

Lyman explained that TAMUP's total dedicated resources from university sources had been a $200,000 account—supplemented by private donations from many former students and other entities. By 1981, that $200,000 fund had been used to publish sixty-eight titles, which translated into an average publication subsidy for each book of $1,700. Lyman informed the board that, in order to maintain the kind of momentum the press had developed, supplemental funds had to be provided for continuing publications—meanwhile, the press would continue to search for grants and funds from sources outside the university. The board approved the press's $200,000 minute order.[40]

What is remarkable about the approval of these funds is not that Lyman's 1981 letter to Hubert and his personal appeal to the regents seem to have had results. Rather, it is remarkable that Frank Hubert asked Lyman to produce a letter justifying additional funding for TAMUP operations, and asked him to present the case to the Board of Regents. As chancellor, Hubert took strong steps to provide a permanent home for the university press and to double the original amount allocated to its general operating funds revolving account.

In March, 1981, Hubert announced that he would be retiring as interim chancellor. Soon after this, TAMU President Charles Samson announced that he too would be retiring. In August, 1981, following an intensive search for a new president, Hubert contacted Frank E. Vandiver and asked him if he would come and interview for the position. Vandiver had not been a candidate for the position, but, after consulting with others, he agreed to consider the job. He already was familiar with the university through his associations with Texas A&M University Press, as both an author and a member of the press's Advisory Council. On September 1, 1981, the Board of Regents made Vandiver president of Texas A&M University. One of his first official acts was to have TAMUP reassigned from the chancellor's purview to that of the president. Some changes in the press staff also took place.

Bill Shearer, who had worked closely with Gayla Christiansen to build a broad sales base for TAMUP books across Texas, left the press in 1981 to start his own business, Shearer Publishing Company. Lyman remembers that, when Shearer left, the staff responded as though there had been a death in the family. Headquartered at first in Bryan, Shearer soon purchased a small press—Shoal Creek Publishers—and moved his home and offices into a century-old, two-story German stone farmhouse and adjoining beer and dance hall in Fredericksburg, Texas. To his new enterprise, Shearer brought an intense love of books, an intuitive sense of the regional book market, an understanding of book publishing gleaned in good measure from his associations with Frank Wardlaw and Lloyd Lyman, and unusual degrees of resourcefulness and resolution.[41]

In time, Shearer's small press prospered. With the blessings and good will of the Texas A&M University Press and his many acquaintances in Texas publishing and bookmaking, he extended the folksy, personal, regional style developed by Wardlaw into the world of commercial publishing. His authors included such notable Texas writers as Jack Maguire, Cactus Pryor, Leon Hale, and Lou Rodenberger. Shearer published fiction, cookbooks, poetry, reminiscences, and a successful travel "roads" series—books largely outside the realm of university publishing but still in the spirit of Texas regionalism.

Tragically, Shearer's life was cut short. He died in 1996, at the age of forty-five, after wrestling mightily with a cancerous brain tumor. His friends remarked that "he was a rare and singular blend of romantic and doer" and that he had "a keen instinct for markets and the business discipline to make it all go."[42] Shearer truly enjoyed people, stories, books, Texas A&M, and life in general. He was one of the remarkable and dedicated people who contributed greatly to the inception and early development of the Texas A&M Press.

TAMUP came into being in years when the techniques and technology of publishing were in flux and when book marketing and distribution methods were changing rapidly. As one of Shearer's friends commented in his eulogy, "When a bad economy and the giant bookstore chains began to radically change bookselling and publishing, it affected us all. Independent bookstores died or had to reinvent themselves. Similarly, [in its short lifetime,] Shearer Publishing had to rethink the kind of books it would publish, the kind of books the public would buy."[43] TAMUP, too, was tied to the marketplace, as well as to the vicissitudes of academia.

In March, 1982, the Board of Regents named Arthur Hansen, an engineer and former president of Purdue University, chancellor of the A&M University System. After some years of administrative turbulence, stability began to return to the campus and to the press.

By late 1982, the affairs of the press had begun to improve. A new building was under construction. More money was now available for publications, and the publication list was being expanded. Revenues from book sales soon began to show a dramatic increase, as is shown in Table 1. Income from sales had tripled in nine years, and the press now could boast of an impressive backlog of titles in the warehouse.

Progress on the new building meant that the staff had to pay more and more attention to myriad major and minor construction details. Were electrical outlets in the right places? Were computer outlets correctly located? Had the proper furnishings been ordered? Why, in September, had a sufficient number of storage racks (pallets) for the warehouse not been approved and ordered by the Office of Facilities Planning and Construction? Without the racks, warehouse space would be virtually useless. One regent objected strongly to the architects' plan for placing an open-air atrium in the center of the building, since this would be a waste of usable space. At the regent's instigation, the architects decided to roof the proposed atrium and use the space for offices.[44]

TABLE 1

Texas A&M University Press

Net Sales by Fiscal Years, 1975–76 to 1983–84

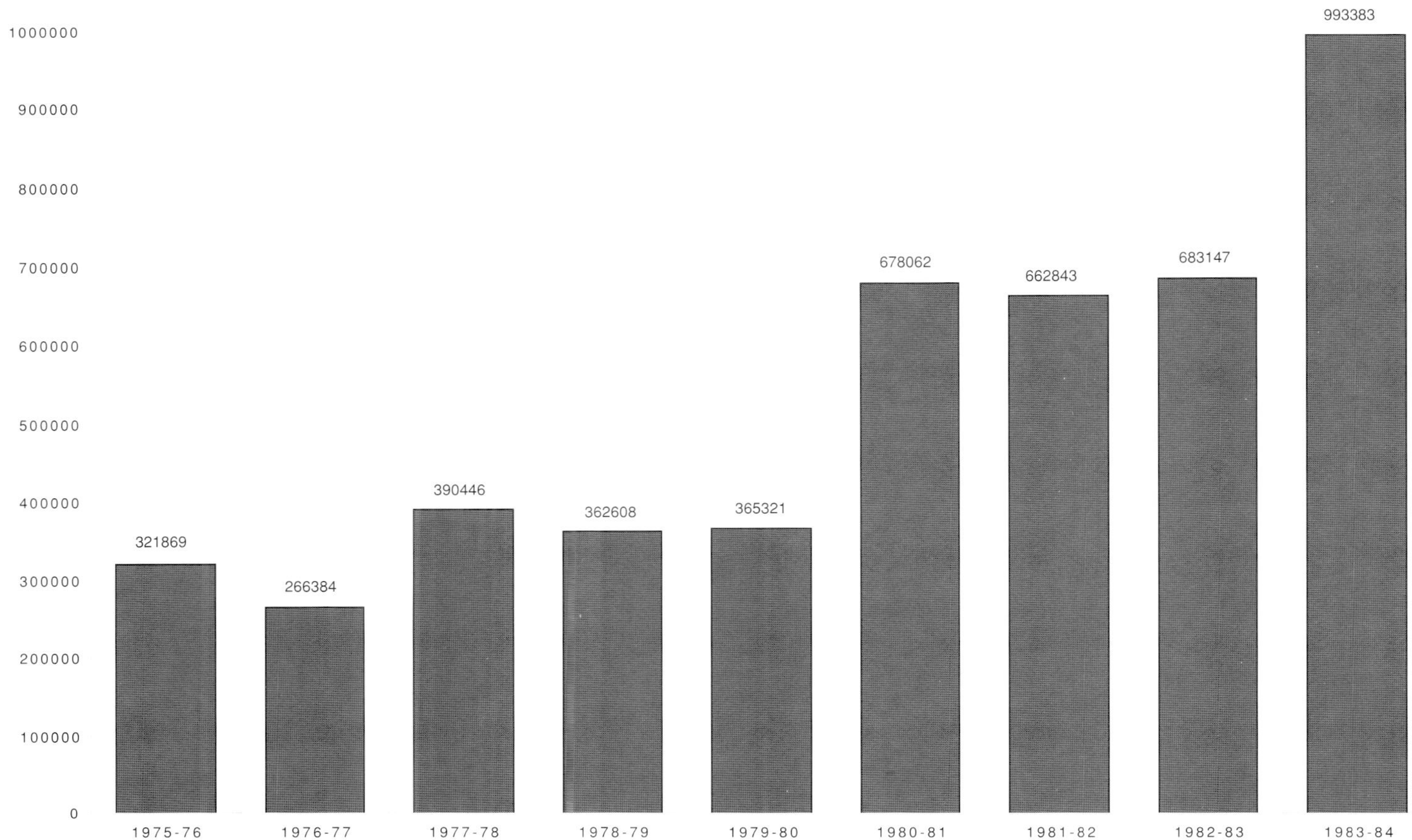

The question soon arose: what (or for whom) would the new building be named? Naming became an important consideration as the building neared completion in the spring of 1983. Lyman responded enthusiastically to a suggestion by Joe Moore and others that the new building be named for Frank Wardlaw. Lyman initiated a vigorous letter-writing campaign to the Advisory Council, selected former students, members of the Faculty Advisory Committee, A&M administrators, friends, and others requesting suggestions for a name for the new facility. Responses overwhelmingly supported naming it the Frank Wardlaw Texas A&M University Press Building. John Lindsey gave his enthusiastic support to naming the building for Wardlaw, since "without him we could never be where we are today." (Lindsey tactfully added, "Without you [Lyman] we would not be where we are either.") Frank Vandiver, in his capacity as a member of the Advisory Council rather than as university president, also responded favorably: "It was Frank's initiative and leadership that got the press going, and it is most fitting that the building be named for him."[45]

The Board of Regents, however, had other ideas. Sterling C. Evans wrote to Lyman that, before he heard about the interest in naming the building for Wardlaw, he already had suggested the name of John Lindsey for the new building. "I did this because he had been the first one to support the idea of having a Press and was instrumental in getting the University to employ Mr. Frank H. Wardlaw as the first director to head that program." Evans regretted finding himself in conflict with Joe Moore's suggestion, because "I can't think of anyone who is as interested in the welfare of the University and who has contributed as much to its success as he has in the years since he was a student there."[46]

Shortly after the staff completed its move, and on the afternoon before the A&M–Arkansas State football game of September 17, 1983, Texas A&M University dedicated the John H. Lindsey Texas A&M University Press Building.[47]

Director Lyman presided while H. R. (Bum) Bright, chairman of the Board of Regents, presented the building, and Chancellor Arthur G. Hansen accepted it on behalf of the administration. On behalf of the State of Texas, two state senators who had been members of A&M's Class of 1974 acknowledged the establishment of TAMUP and the dedication of the Lindsey Building. State Sen. Kent A. Caperton (former student body president and

FIG. 23. *Jack K. Williams and Frank Wardlaw chat with E. M. "Buck" Schiwetz at the dedication of the John H. Lindsey Building and the Wardlaw Art Collection in September 1983.*

onetime aide to President Jack K. Williams) and State Sen. Chet Edwards (who later served in the U.S. House of Representatives) remarked:

> *First there must be a dream, and then the prescience to recognize how to make that dream a reality. Already a distinguished former student with an impressive list of contributions to Texas A&M, John Lindsey nurtured his dream to bring scholarly publishing to Aggieland, [and] then, when the chance came to make that dream come true he took it. Today, the university and its press are indebted to him for his devotion to that dream and for enduring commitment to Texas A&M and the University Press.*[48]

Frank Wardlaw, called back to College Station from his Fripp Island retirement home, joined in extending this honor to John Lindsey, and he in turn shared that honor. Perhaps still somewhat nostalgic about the press's quarters in the Old Board of Directors Building, he quipped, "The old building had seventeen bathrooms, and was the most commodious press building in the United States."[49] The new building had neither such numerous nor such commodious facilities, but by any measure it was one of the largest and best appointed university press buildings in the nation.

FIG. 24. *During a visit by Frank Wardlaw to College Station in the summer of 1984, the press staff gathered to have their photograph made with him in the press conference room.*

Unknown to Wardlaw and in response to suggestions made by the press staff, Lyman quickly redirected the enthusiasm for naming the new building after Wardlaw into a movement to create the Frank H. Wardlaw Collection of Texas Art, which would be displayed permanently in the press's new home. Lyman had conducted another intensive letter-writing campaign—this time to Texas artists and friends of Wardlaw whose work had been included in TAMUP books, asking their help in establishing the collection in his honor. Twenty paintings by nineteen prominent Texas artists were donated to the press. The collection included a lithograph by John Thomas Biggers, a noted African American artist at Texas Southern University. Jerry Bywaters, Southern Methodist University artist and professor emeritus, contributed a watercolor of Texas bunkhouses. Wardlaw long had relied upon the advice and assistance of Bywaters, who had served as director of the Dallas Museum of Fine Arts from 1942 to 1963. Finis F. Collins (a founding member of the Watercolor Gang) contributed a picture of a windmill, while Michael Frary offered a Gulf Coast scene and a painting of a century plant. E. M. "Buck" Schiwetz's original drawing of "Gathright Hall" was presented to John Lindsey during the dedication ceremonies. Other Texas artists with works in the

Wardlaw Collection included Marbury Hill Brown, Otis Dozier, Kelly Fearing, Frank Gervasi, John William Guerin, William Hoey, William Lester, Ivan Ellis McDougal, Ancel Nunn, Harold Phenix, Stephen T. Rascoe, Mondel Rogers, Emily Guthrie Smith, Everett Franklin Spruce, and E. Gordon West.[50]

Concurrent with the dedication of the John H. Lindsey Building and the Wardlaw Art Collection, the A&M Press announced publication of the

FIG. 25. *Artists and art teachers John Biggers and Carroll Simms were influential in establishing a highly respected art program at Texas Southern University. In 1978 the press published their story, written with John Edward Weems, in the book* Black Art in Houston: The Texas Southern University Experience. *This mural,* Harvest Song, *is by John Biggers.*

FIG. 26. *Texas artists Finis F. Collins* (left) *and Ivan McDougal at the Lindsey Building dedication. Both artists contributed works to the Wardlaw Art Collection, housed in the building. The painting shown here is Collins's "Windmill," a 1983 watercolor. McDougal's contribution to the collection was "Sunset of an Era—Mineowner's Mansion, Terlingua."*

sixth title in the Joe and Betty Moore Texas Art Series, *Pecos to the Rio Grande: Interpretations of Far West Texas by Eighteen Artists.* The book contained an introduction by Ron Tyler and a foreword by Frank H. Wardlaw.

Wardlaw's friends and colleagues from the world of university publishing also announced the creation of a publication fund in his honor. "It seems appropriate," wrote Chester Kerr (former director of Yale University Press), August Frugé (former director of the University of California Press), Jack Schulman (former director of Cambridge University Press), and Jack Goellner (director of Johns Hopkins University Press), "to paint his name into the College Station landscape in yet another set of colors. With the aid of the annual income from such a Fund, it ought to be possible, even with such a modest beginning [$2,500], for the Press to publish a new book every two or three years which might not otherwise be economically feasible."[51] The first three Wardlaw Books would be published in 1985, an event celebrated with a grand party in Austin at the Hirshfeld-Moore House, which had recently been given to Texas A&M University by Joe and Betty Moore.

Finally, and fittingly, the dedication of the new John H. Lindsey Texas A&M University Press Building received front-page billing in the Texas A&M–Arkansas State football game program. It was, by any measure, a most successful occasion.

The dedication of the new building marked a watershed, a new beginning for the Texas A&M University Press. But it also signaled the end of what might be called "the charismatic age"—if the press might be believed to have had such—and the beginning of the institutional, or mature, phase. While work and life in the trailer units had created stresses and strains, that same environment had forced upon the staff a closeness that never would be equaled again. Much as frontier hardships had created special bonds among early settlers, the constricted space of the trailers had enhanced the staff's sense of being a team. Lyman consistently encouraged staff involvement in decision making; under his direction, as during Frank Wardlaw's tenure, duties were relatively uncompartmentalized. Everyone was willing to do whatever needed to be done.

Now, curiously, things would be different. The very spaciousness of the new quarters, as well as the floor plan's departmental emphasis, invited compartmentalization and heightened the sense of formality. The new building changed the tenor of the place. Organizational dynamics changed. Sales and income grew; to a lesser extent, the staff began to grow, too, in accord with the increased number of books being produced and distributed. The small, traditional, charismatic, regional, Wardlaw-style press was evolving into a larger institutional operation. This latter, while retaining a strong regional base, incorporated a national and international dimension reflecting the remarkable growth and transformation of its parent university.[52]

Texas A&M University was a school where things could happen. The new president, Frank E. Vandiver, had a vision for A&M: it could become a true "world-class university," and it should build to accommodate the new global society. The Texas A&M Press would be a handmaiden to the university in its developing role. This meant that the press, like the larger institution, would be subjected to demanding evaluations and testing from within and from without. The press's primary role, however, continued to be, as it had been since the beginning, to extend the educational mission of Texas A&M University into new territory.

Chapter 4

MAKING BOOKS

The book is the coin of the realm of ideas. Books give ideas and information a physical reality in a format that is compact, reasonably durable, relatively inexpensive, and easily transferable. A university press is a university-related service industry. The service provided is making books, a task that lies in the penumbra between art and craft. Bookmaking includes finding and often nurturing an author; testing, refining, evaluating, and certifying the author's ideas; editing, designing, and printing the written work; advertising, selling, and distributing the product—and generating an income sufficient to sustain these operations. A university press serves two masters: the scholarly and university community and the publishing industry.

Manuscripts do not spring spontaneously from the academic or human intellect. They must be solicited, encouraged, nourished, sometimes even demanded. In the half-century following World War II, society began to require manuscripts of its scholars. Federal, state, and foundation expenditures for education, research, and development grew, while a more broadly educated society seemed to hunger insatiably for more and better information and science. Within this climate, increasingly the motto of the academy in the United States became "publish or perish." Faculty generally both wanted and needed to write books.

Thus Texas A&M University Press grew up in a world clamoring for more books, amid a growing host of aspiring authors. Quality, selection, responsibility, and credibility became even more critical in the expanding

FIG. 27. *Lady Bird Johnson autographs copies of* Texas in Bloom *while Joe and Betty Moore look on during a book signing in Austin soon after the book's release.*

world of university publishing. In some ways, publishing became an easier task, but publishing *good* books that provided comprehensible and credible information became more difficult. Selection became crucial. For every book TAMUP published, numerous manuscripts were rejected. A press's credibility can be tested by the books it has avoided publishing, as well as by the books featured in its catalog.

Throughout the publishing industry, bookmaking had become increasingly competitive, stimulating the publication of more books but also increasing the tension between quantity and quality. As pressures to publish rose and as universities—such as Texas A&M University—increasingly sought to amplify their reputations and their prestige, university publishing tended to encounter heightened political and partisan pressures from faculty and administrators. It was very important to TAMUP's integrity that it be insulated from campus politics and granted an unusual degree of independence within the academic system. The A&M Press's revolving accounts reduced dependence upon university funding and enhanced its independence, integrity, and credibility. Frank Wardlaw, with the support of Jack Williams, other administrators, and the Association of Former Students, positioned the press so that it enjoyed an unusual degree of independence in other areas. Joe and Betty Moore, for example, who had endowed a book series, understood that their generous gifts provided no license to control or advise—and they preferred it that way.

Jimmy Carlysle (Jim) Billingsley, who joined TAMUP as design and production editor in 1986, thought that, compared with the other university presses with which he was familiar, the A&M Press enjoyed an unusual degree of independence and integrity and also was very well financed. "Support was staggering," he recalled, "and the University provided us with what we needed to do the job."[1]

Billingsley replaced Ray Grimaila, who was ill for some time before his death in the summer of 1985. As book production began to rise in the early 1980s, design manager Grimaila occasionally turned to Billingsley for freelance assistance in the design of books, although most of the design work continued to be done in-house. Once a design was completed, Grimaila would send the project out for composition, printing, and binding by suppliers chosen under Texas' competitive bidding procedures. Each book had unique design and layout characteristics. When part of a series, a book's design would also reflect the character of the series.[2]

The printer was an important element in the bookmaking process. A printer often possessed special competencies that suited a particular kind or style of book. Over time, TAMUP developed close relationships with a number of suppliers, such as Hart Graphics of Austin, Texas; and Thomson-Shore, Inc., of Dexter, Michigan. High quality in design, appearance, and print remained the standard for book production.

Because of his working association with Grimaila, Billingsley provided a relatively easy transition when he arrived in College Station in the spring of 1986.[3] Billingsley, who grew up in Tulsa, was born in Sapulpa, Oklahoma, a small town given visibility by its local railroad telegrapher, Gene Autry, who went on to fame and fortune as a star in early Western movies. Sapulpa also is the home of the famed Frankoma Pottery. Curiously, Sapulpa was the birthplace of two men who achieved considerable recognition as university press design artists and editors—B. J. Conkwright, who became art editor at the University of Oklahoma Press and later design chief at Princeton University Press; and Billingsley, whose career included tenures at the University of Oklahoma Press, the University of Tennessee Press, and Texas A&M University Press.

Billingsley's education had been interrupted by military service during the Korean War. Thereafter, he completed his degree in commercial art and journalism at the University of Tulsa and worked for some years as an oil-field cartographer and production draftsman. In 1962, while working as a commercial artist for DX Sunray Oil Company, Billingsley was intrigued by an advertisement for an assistant art editor at the University of Oklahoma Press.[4]

He submitted an application and was hired. He thoroughly enjoyed the work under press director Savoie Lottinville, focusing on American Indian, Latin American, and Western titles. In 1968, Billingsley accepted the position of design editor at the University of Tennessee Press under Louis Iglehart. The Tennessee press had been established in 1942 but had languished until the administration decided in the 1960s to rejuvenate it. Billingsley performed yeoman service in that rejuvenation during his many years at Tennessee.[5]

When Lloyd Lyman asked him to consider coming to TAMUP to replace Grimaila, Billingsley again was intrigued. He visited the campus and liked what he saw. People, he recalled, could not have been nicer. Moreover, there was a lot to be done. There was a backlog of work, and the greater diversity in the character of books at the Texas A&M University Press presented a challenge and an opportunity for a design artist. Billingsley plunged into his work at TAMUP with enthusiasm.

One of Billingsley's first (and perhaps his most memorable) experience in design and production there had to do with a book by the Texas artist and illustrator, Tom Lea. A close friend of Frank Wardlaw, Lea—who had designed the TAMUP logo—was, according to the book's dust jacket, a southwestern "artist, muralist, painter, book illustrator, World War II artist-correspondent, historian, novelist, humanist, and philosopher." Lea's books included an illustrated history of the King Ranch and a popular novel, *The Wonderful Country.* Lea collaborated with J. Frank Dobie on many books, including the classic *Apache Gold and Yaqui Silver.*

In 1939, in a letter to Lea following publication of *Apache Gold,* Dobie explained the role of the illustrator and by inference that of the design editor in the bookmaking process: "[The illustrations] not only illustrate incident, character and country but interpret, bring out significance, and vivify." In selecting the type style, illustrations, and overall composition, the design editor helped to create the book. Thus, in some ways, Dobie noted, *Apache Gold* "does not seem my work at all, but Tom Lea's aided by the art and craft of printing."[6] Design was an integral but often misunderstood part of making books.

Working with Lea, Billingsley recalled, was "a little frightening at first" but turned out to be a wonderful experience. Lea carefully examined every line and weighed each element of the book. Production took time. The book came into the press's offices in 1986 and appeared in print in 1989. Publication was funded by a generous grant from the Robert J. Kleberg, Jr., and Helen C. Kleberg Foundation "in honor of the longtime friendship between Tom Lea and Robert J. Kleberg, Jr."[7]

In his overall management, Lloyd Lyman, as director of TAMUP, provided oversight but generally stayed out of the production loop. Lyman focused on manuscript acquisition and review and worked energetically to seek new funds and other resources for the press. Placing great confidence in each staff member, he invited and welcomed decisions by the staff. With the decisions came accountability, however. Lyman delegated greater authority to the staff and gave them more independence than Wardlaw had.[8] The work grew with the press.

The Faculty Advisory Committee's role became more clearly defined and more integral to the publishing process. Clinton A. Phillips replaced Haskell Monroe as dean of faculties and chair of the FAC in 1980, when Monroe accepted an appointment as president of the University of Texas at El Paso. (After service at UTEP, Monroe became chancellor of the University of Missouri at Columbia.) Phillips—a professor of finance, a former department head, and acting dean of the College of Business Administration at the time of his promotion—chaired the FAC for the next fifteen years. During that time, he not only provided direction and counsel, but also helped to weave the faculty at large into the fabric of the press.

Phillips, like others who served on this committee, counted it as one of his most satisfying university duties. In 1983, FAC members and their scholarly affiliations included: Robert A. Albanese (management), Vaughn Bryant (sociology and anthropology), Thomas C. Cartwright (animal science), Elenor R. Cox (biology), Henry C. Dethloff (history), Donald Dyal (special collections), Jerry Gibson (electrical engineering), Sylvia Grider (English), Kenneth R. Hall (chemical engineering), Russell C. Long (English, Tarleton State University), S. Charles Maurice (economics), Campbell W. Pennington (geography), Phillips (business), Frank Pierce (English), Joseph Pratt (history), Alvin A. Price (veterinary physiology and pharmacology), Sammy Ray (marine technology, TAMU Galveston), David Schmidly (wildlife sciences), William P. Snyder (political science), Gene C. Uselton (executive development), and David Woodcock (architecture). Members served a three-year term, with many repeating for consecutive terms. Meetings usually involved six or eight members, selected for their particular expertise or interest in the subjects of the manuscripts under consideration. The committee assisted not only in the making of books, but also helped integrate the press into the university community by soliciting manuscripts, serving as ombudsmen between the faculty and TAMUP, and by keeping the press's editors informed about the academic and literary activities of faculty members.

The FAC and the press staff often began work on a book years in advance of its publication. For example, in 1983, the committee considered and approved for publication a manuscript still in progress, *Halford Mackinder: A Biography,* by Brian W. Blouet; it did not appear in print until 1987. Authors T. Lindsay Baker and Billy R. Harrison first handed *Adobe Walls: The History and Archeology of the 1874 Trading Post* to Lloyd Lyman in 1981. Lyman and the staff reviewed the manuscript, returned it to the authors for revisions, and then submitted it to the FAC for approval in 1983; after further revisions, it was published in 1986.[9]

Making scholarly books was long-term work. In the fall of 1985, the press announced the beginning of two new series. One, entitled Tarleton State University Southwestern Studies in the Humanities, was established under the editorial direction of William T. (Tom) Pilkington and featured studies in southwestern literature and popular and fine arts. Dr. Barry Thompson, president of Tarleton State University (who in 1994 would become chancellor of the Texas A&M University System) was the catalyst for Tarleton's association with the A&M Press. The first book to appear in the Southwestern Studies series was *In the Deep Heart's Core: Reflections on Life, Letters, and Texas,* by Craig Edward Clifford, a writer and professor of English at Tarleton State, who represented a new generation of Texas writers.[10]

The second new series was to be a reprint series under the rubric Southwest Landmarks. The first book published in the series was Larry McMurtry's widely acclaimed first novel, *Horseman, Pass By,* originally published in 1961. From that work, McMurtry went on to write many award-winning novels, including *The Last Picture Show, Leaving Cheyenne, Somebody's Darling, Terms of Endearment,* and *Lonesome Dove.* In the spring of 1986, the press released a second McMurtry novel, *Leaving Cheyenne,* as part of the same series.[11] McMurtry's work epitomized the transition from old frontier to new, and his writing has continued to mirror the changing world of the West, the South, the Southwest, and Texas.

Texas A&M Press publications increasingly reflected the transition from the West of Webb, Dobie, Lea, and Zane Grey, to the West of *Early California Oil: A Photographic History, 1865–1940,* by Kenny A. Franks and Paul F. Lambert (Kenneth E. Montague Series in Oil and Business History, 1985); and of William D. Rowley, who, in *U.S. Forest Service Grazing and Rangeland* (1985), critically discussed the history of government control of western grazing lands.[12] Some of the complexities of western change were captured in *The Chief: Ernest Thompson Seton and the Changing West* (1986). Seton was hostile to modern technology and sought a "peaceful relationship" with nature. Unintentionally, he contributed to the development of the Boy Scouts of America and the modern environmental movement. The influence of technology on the West was explored further in Don L. Hofsommer's history, *The Southern Pacific, 1901–1985,* published in 1986; and in T. Lindsay Baker's *Building the Lone Star: An Illustrated Guide to Historic Sites,* which emphasized engineering aspects of construction of various sites, including the Galveston Sea Wall. Concurrently, the press released a book in the Tarleton Southwestern Studies series, *Cannibals and Condos,* a study of the changes and human costs associated with modern development along the Texas Gulf Coast.[13]

FIG. 28. *Texas Christian University professor Jim Corder wrote and illustrated* Lost in West Texas *in the mid-1980s, and the press published it in 1988. The book's delightful mixture of nostalgia, wonderment, and imagination are evidenced by this drawing of a West Texas homestead.*

But Also Good Business, a hundred-year history of Texas Commerce Bank, written by Walter L. Buenger and Joseph A. Pratt, argued that at the heart of modern Texas were the banks and the flow of credit that had fed the spectacular financial growth of Houston and the rest of the state since World War II.[14] Published in 1986, this book appeared at the height of the state's financial expansion—and on the eve of a deep and pervasive financial and banking collapse that began in 1987. Texas and the Southwest were changing. Texas A&M University Press was evolving, too.

Mary Ann Flusche Jacob joined the press staff in 1985 to work with Gayla Christiansen in the marketing department. A native of Austin with a degree in studio art from the University of Texas, Jacob later worked in the graphic design department of the Texas House of Representatives. After her marriage, she and her husband moved to College Station. She worked for a time in the Texas A&M University Printing Center and did some freelance advertising design for TAMUP. In 1985, she joined the press to focus full-time on advertising and catalog planning and design.[15]

The year after Jacob's arrival, a vacancy developed for a design assistant to help Jim Billingsley. Jacob encouraged Susan Pettey, who had worked with her at the A&M Printing Center, to apply for the position. Pettey had grown up in Waco and attended what was then Texas State Technical College, where she received her degree in graphic arts in 1981. In June, 1986, she began work at TAMUP with Billingsley. While she had some idea of what publishing entailed—her family had run a weekly newspaper in Jewett, Texas, for more than one hundred years—Pettey found the work both new and exciting, a real challenge. Each person had a lot of independence, Susan observed, but at the same time "everyone at some time 'touches' every book."[16] Making books clearly was a team effort.

When Don Collins left TAMUP, Lyman promoted Collins's former assistant, Dianna Hein, to the post of business manager. Hein had joined the press in the early days, on July 1, 1975, as Collins's accounting assistant. Collins had begun work that same day, she recalled. Like most of the staff, Hein became a part of university publishing more by default than by planning. She needed a job, and one was available at the press. In addition, she loved to read books. Hein had begun her business career at the age of fourteen, working as an accounting assistant and office manager for her grandfather. She had developed a diverse business background, receiving special training from special people like Frank Wardlaw and Don Collins. Thus it gave Hein a special sense of accomplishment to become TAMUP business manager in 1986. She was one of the youngest business managers on the campus and among the first females to occupy such a position there.[17]

Production, income, and expenses increased in the mid-1980s, paralleling the growth of the press. Keeping track of the growing distribution lists, sales by associated university presses, and diverse accounts created technological overload at TAMUP. When the press first opened for business, the University of Texas Press handled A&M's orders on its computers. Within a few years, Texas A&M University's Computing Services bureau had adapted Wylbur computer software on the university's mainframe computer to manage accounts. Later, Don Beaugez of Computer Services designed accounting software for use by the press staff on personal computers. Increasing sales resulted in Beaugez's revising and enhancing the press's programs in 1986, but overload and technical obsolescence continued to cause problems. In 1992, the press adopted a sophisticated and highly effective software program called Cat's Pajamas, which was designed especially for the scholarly publishing business and its marketing systems.[18]

TAMUP's growth required not only constantly upgrading technology, but also increasing specialization on the part of staff members. Gradually, the "we do it all" management style gave way to a more departmentalized form. Originally, the business department sold books, took orders, verified invoices, shipped books, paid bills, created budgets, and did whatever else needed to be done. Hein described the press's business management as evolving from "cigar box" accounting to a true financial management system. The "cigar box" referred to Frank Wardlaw's habit of passing around his El Producto cigar box during weekend fundraising parties.[19]

Related to informal cigar-box solicitations was a distinctive social event called "The Gathering of the Herd." This event brought together friends of Wardlaw, John Lindsey, and Joe and Betty Moore—as well as other friends of the A&M Press who enjoyed each other's company and who in some fashion were committed to the press. The Moores were instigators, calling on people such as Lady Bird Johnson to support and attend the gathering. The "Gathering of the Herd" invitations indicated a ranch setting with "dress country casual." In addition to an abundance of solid and liquid refreshments and a surfeit of tall tales, these events included a book auction to benefit the university and "cigar box" collections for TAMUP. John Lindsey recalled the gatherings as unique occasions which helped to create the special mystique associated with Wardlaw and Texas A&M University Press.[20]

Financial management became more sophisticated. Jobs became more specialized. Burgeoning book orders soon required the full-time attention of an individual whose specific responsibility was order fulfillment. Dianna Hein, who soon would replace Don Collins as business manager, helped to recruit Sharon Yvonne Pavlas (now Mills). Pavlas, a native of Bryan, at the time was working as a temporary employee for an oil and gas holding company and wanted full-time employment on the A&M campus. She began work as order fulfillment clerk in May, 1986. While she had had little knowledge of, or interest in, publishing before she began working at the press, it "grew" on her, even as her position grew. Order fulfillment became a separate department in 1993, with Pavlas as manager. Her job was not merely to fill book orders, but also to provide assistance to distribution clients such as TCU, SMU, and the Texas State Historical Association. Distribution work often involved providing marketing and pricing advice, as well as managing orders. Pavlas produced monthly reports for the associated presses, detailing sales, receivables, returns, and inventories, as well as a monthly check. She remembered the remarkable growth of TAMUP during this period: "We were so small in 1986; we labored to generate $50,000 in book sales a month. Within ten years we were anticipating monthly sales of $200,000."[21] Things indeed were changing.

TAMUP expanded its series publishing. The fall of 1986 saw the beginning of the Clayton Wheat Williams Texas Life Series, funded by Clayton ("Claytie") W. Williams, Jr., who had amassed a fortune in the oil business following the OPEC embargo. He had a strong personal interest in Texas A&M and in Texas history and life. In 1982, the press had published a book written by his father, Clayton W. Williams, entitled *Texas' Last Frontier: Fort Stockton and the Trans-Pecos, 1861–1895,* edited by historian Ernest Wallace. The senior Williams had been born in the old officers' quarters at Fort Stockton in 1895. Although active in ranching and the oil business, his deep interest in history led him to writing and to a term as president of the West Texas Historical Association.[22]

Williams, Jr., shared his father's interest in history and his love of Texas. Seeking to focus on "everyday life in the Lone Star State from the beginning of recorded history to modern times," the Texas Life series was based on the premise that "how people determine their means and style of existence dictates history—the outbreak and duration of wars, the depth of peace, and the management of prosperity."[23]

The first book in the new series was a nostalgic view of the rural past, *Plantation Life in Texas,* by Elizabeth A. Silverthorne. Charles Shaw, the illustrator, working with TAMUP design manager Billingsley, captured the essence of the book in a number of accurately detailed illustrations, including one published on the cover. Joe and Betty Moore hosted a "Plantation Party" to celebrate both publication of the book and announcement of the new series.

The famous author, James A. Michener, helped to inspire the Texas Life Series. Michener's books included *Tales of the South Pacific, Return to Paradise, The Voice of Asia, The Bridges of Toko-Ri,* and *Sayonara*—all written in the aftermath of his World War II experiences in the South Pacific. *Centennial, Chesapeake, The Covenant, Space, Poland,* and other popular titles followed over the years. Michener had returned to Texas late in 1982 to begin work on another of his epic novels—one entitled simply *Texas.* While at work on *Texas,* Michener lived in Austin and focused his research efforts on the library and archival resources at the University of Texas. In the course of his research, he became acquainted with Joe Moore and Clayton Williams, Jr., both of whom provided personal insights into the evolution of Texas' petroleum industry. On a number of occasions, the pair also provided Michener with transportation (airplanes and helicopters). Although Michener declined because of its rather remote location, Joe and Betty Moore also offered Michener the use of one of their houses. On one occasion, Joe Moore and Michener flew out to West Texas with Jack Williams to attend one of Clayton Williams's bull sales. Soon after that event, Michener called Moore to say that he wanted to visit Texas A&M. In College Station, the novelist received an enthusiastic welcome. During his visit, he interviewed some local people as well as university faculty and TAMUP staff.[24]

During one of their conversations, Michener suggested to Lloyd Lyman that TAMUP consider publishing a series of books devoted to aspects of daily life during the various periods of Texas history, from the time of the Spanish missions to the present. It should be a "mud-sills" social history, he suggested. He also recommended that Lyman approach all the heads of history departments at various Texas colleges and universities, as well as the staff of the Barker History Center, the Texas Institute of Learning, and the Texas State Historical Association, inviting their participation and assistance in establishing this series.[25]

At the Texas–Texas A&M football game in College Station in November, 1983, Lyman discussed the Michener proposal with Clayton Williams, Jr. A&M beat Texas, and Williams agreed to support the Texas Life Series. A few days after the game, Williams wrote to Bob Walker, director of the Office of University Development, "Thanks to you and the Texas A&M football team, Modesta and I had one hell of a weekend, even if it was expensive." That weekend Williams had committed $50,000 for the development of an embryo transfer station for ungulates for the College of Veterinary Medicine and another $150,000 to fund the Clayton Wheat Williams Texas Life Series. "I know my dad would be absolutely delighted at such a perpetual and ongoing acknowledgment in his memory to the 'History of Texas.' "[26]

The second publication in the Texas Life Series, Robert Wooster's *Soldiers, Sutlers, and Settlers,* traces the interaction of life on the frontier with the life lived in protective military outposts.

This work complemented a veritable stream of military history books

FIG. 29. East of Chosin: Entrapment and Breakout in Korea, 1950, *became the second volume in the press's Military History Series in 1987 and has become one of the press's military history best-sellers. By retired army lieutenant colonel Roy Appleman, the book tells the tragic story of a disastrous retreat across the frozen Chosin Reservoir during the Korean War.*

published in TAMUP's Military History Series, beginning in 1987 with several gripping volumes: Weldon E. ("Dusty") Rhoades, *Flying MacArthur to Victory;* Roy E. Appleman's *East of Chosin,* outlining the entrapment of American military forces in Korea; Klaus H. Huebner's *Long Walk Through War: A Combat Doctor's Diary,* kept by an American battalion physician with the 88th Infantry Division during the French and Italian campaigns in World War II; and William L. Richter's *The Army in Texas During Reconstruction.* TAMU President Frank E. Vandiver's *Their Tattered Flags: The Epic of the Confederacy* (which one reviewer said was "written with the pace of a Confederate infantry charge") also appeared in 1987 (and was reprinted in 1988,1990, and 1995), while his *Mighty Stonewall* appeared in 1988 (and was reprinted in 1989, 1992, and 1995).[27]

In 1987, the press announced the publication of fifteen new titles in the spring, and another fifteen in the fall (almost double the level of production anticipated by Wardlaw ten years earlier), with an additional assortment of paperback reprints and a healthy list of publications by consortium member presses—Southern Methodist University Press, Rice University Press, Texas Christian University Press, and the Texas State Historical Association.

Between 1984 and 1987, the Moody Foundation, which earlier had funded the W. L. Moody, Jr., Natural History Series, provided independent publishing subventions for three books authored by Douglas Caddy, a Houston attorney, and through those endowments established new capital accounts for the publication of TAMUP books. The first of the titles was a brief overview and a consumer guide, *Understanding Texas Insurance,* published in 1984. The Moody Foundation existed largely because of family insurance and shipping businesses. The second book, published in 1986, was *Legislative Trends in Insurance Regulation* (with a focus on Texas), and the third was *Exploring America's Future,* in which Caddy discussed events and trends of the past few decades and projected changes that might be anticipated in family, education, religion, technology, and world power structures.[28]

Sometimes the thread leading to the endowment of a book series was thin and fragile. Such was the case in the development of the Charles and Elizabeth Prothro Texas Photography Series. The series stemmed from a comment made to Lloyd Lyman by a commissioner of the Texas Historical Commission, that excellent photographs for book publications were abundantly available in that agency's collections. Subsequently, William Wright of Abilene suggested that Elizabeth Prothro might be interested in providing financial assistance for publication of a photographic series. Wright introduced Lyman and Noel Parsons to the Prothros in 1986. The Prothros were interested but not committed. In time, Lyman and Parsons brought to their attention two photographic projects (pictures and accompanying narratives) being developed, respectively, by Anne Noggle and June Van Cleef. The Noggle project was the illustrated story of American women Army Air Force service pilots during World War II, a little-known but fascinating story of women in the military. Van Cleef's study dealt with the vanishing of small-town Texas life, as exemplified by the experiences of Hamilton, Texas. The Prothros became very interested and agreed to provide a fund for the establishment of a photographic series. With the Prothros' support, the

FIG. 30. *One of the volumes of historic photography in the Charles and Elizabeth Prothro Texas Photography Series is* Equal before the Lens: Jno. Trlica's Photographs of Granger, Texas *(1992), by Barbara McCandless.*

new series began to take form. Although the groundwork had been laid in 1986, the first volume of the series—Noggle's *For God, Country, and the Thrill of It: Women Air Force Service Pilots in World War II*—did not appear in print until 1990.[29] This special book was followed in 1991 by *Coming to Terms: The German Hill Country of Texas* by Wendy Watriss and Fred Baldwin; and in 1992 by Van Cleef's *The Way Home: Photographs from the Heart of Texas.*[30]

Texas A&M University, once an all-male military institution, in 1971 had changed its admission policy to provide fully and equally for the admission of women. Reflecting this shift as well as changes in American society, the press's publication lists increasingly featured books specifically dealing with women. Julia K. Blackwelder's *Women of the Depression: Caste and Culture in San Antonio, 1929–1939*, published in 1984, was one of the first scholarly studies of Texas women; it broke new ground by integrating class and racial/ethnic dimensions with gender questions. *Texas Tears and Texas Sunshine: Voices of Frontier Women*, edited by Jo Ella Powell Exley and published in 1985 (and reprinted in 1985 and 1986), illuminated Texas frontier conditions with a contemporary feminist perspective. In 1986 and 1987, a number of manuscripts about women began to wend their way through the publication process. The result, in 1988, was a number of interesting and significant new books. Diane Koos Gentry's *Enduring Women* documented the working lives of ten women whose careers included ranching, operating a shrimp boat, mining coal, midwifery, and migrant farm work.[31] *Brush Country Woman*, by Ada Morehead Holland, recounted the life story of an independent spirit, Helen Sewell Harbison, who taught school, served as a county and district clerk, became the wife of a Texas Ranger, raised a large family, and then operated the family ranch for thirty years after the death of her husband, Pell Harbison. *Cavalry Wife: The Diary of Eveline M. Alexander, 1866–1867*, edited by Sandra L. Myers, chronicled the adventures and misadventures of frontier life in New Mexico from the point of view of an army wife.[32] The list of women's studies, history, and lore continued to grow.

Architecture long had been on the A&M Press's list of preferred topics. Both Wardlaw and Lyman worked tirelessly, but with little success, to secure funds for a Texas architecture series. Despite the publication (in the Centennial History Series) and subsequent strong sales of Willard B. Robinson's *Gone from Texas: Our Lost Architectural Heritage* (1981) and the publication of Michael McCullar's *Restoring Texas: Raiford Stripling's Life and Architecture* (1985), the press had done little in the realm of the state's architecture. John and Sara Lindsey helped to meet this need by funding the Sara and John Lindsey Series in the Arts and Humanities.

The first book in the series was Mary Carolyn Hollers George's study of a fascinating southwestern architect, O'Neil Ford. A protégé of David Reichard Williams, a founder of the indigenous southwestern style in architecture, Ford drew upon that background to help create the "Modern" movement in the Southwest, which combined efficiency and economy with regional style. The Ford book project had a history of its own. Willard B.

Robinson, author of *Gone from Texas,* visited with Lyman in 1986 and urged the press to publish a book on Ford. He suggested that the press seek out George, an associate professor of art history at San Antonio College, who then was at work researching Ford. Over several years, work of this scope required financial support from a variety of sources, including the Texas Society of Architects, the San Antonio Conservation Society, and finally a grant from Sara and John Lindsey, administered through the press. In 1986, as a finished manuscript seemed imminent, Sara and John Lindsey donated substantial funds to publish the book, as well as others on similar topics. The release of *O'Neil Ford, Architect* in 1992 illustrates the substantial time and resources sometimes required to bring a book into print.[33]

By 1988, TAMUP was publishing more—many more—books than it had in 1978, when Lyman had become director. Moreover, many of those books (42 of the 325 titles published) had received literary and design awards. These recognitions ranged from Association of American University Presses design and book competitions to awards from the American Association for State and Local History, Westerners International, the Cowboy Hall of Fame and Western Heritage Center, the Texas Historical Commission, the American Society of Mechanical Engineers, the Texas Institute of Letters, the San Antonio Conservation Society, and the Texas State Historical Association. The backlist of titles had risen from 50 in 1978 to more than 325 in 1988. Sales receipts had increased from $50,000 monthly to $200,000 monthly.[34] For Lyman and the staff, these had been exciting, exhausting years.

Now, after ten years, Lyman decided it was time to retire and return to the Oregon coastal town of Bandon, where he and his wife had lived earlier. This area resembled the cool, forested coasts of Lea Lyman's Finnish homeland.[35] On August 28, 1988, a retirement dinner was held in Lyman's honor, hosted by Sara and John Lindsey at the recently opened Clayton W. Williams, Jr., Alumni Center. Frank E. Vandiver (who that same year had announced his own retirement as president of Texas A&M University), in his own eloquent, inimitable style, summarized both Lyman's career as director of TAMUP and the essence of bookmaking. "Publishing," Vandiver said, "is a kind of derring-do. It offers the world a microcosm of thought, of ear and eye, of knowledge torn from nature and from hearts and psyches; it offers comfort, conflict, wisdom, and inanities, sums and substances, dumbness and perversity—all the stuff of life." Great books and bad books, trivia and monuments, all are the stuff of publishing. Vandiver believed that great publishers had become rarer than in the past. The publishing business had become "bottom-line oriented." The "blockbuster book" tended to shove the little treasures aside. The business of the university press was to preserve such treasures, to defend art, life, and scholarship. Great presses do not just happen. They are "the creation of hearts, minds and passions, of dedication, faith and stubborn devotion to quality." Great university press directors stand as the consciences of quality. Lloyd Lyman, Vandiver affirmed, was one of that rare breed. Not only had he continued a great press tradition, but also he had brought it national renown.[36]

At the gathering, Lyman introduced his successor. John Frederick ("Rick") Stetter was a young man, a member of the postwar, post-Depression, unlimited-horizons generation of Americans. He hailed from the West—from Nevada City, California, a place near and not unlike Lyman's hometown of Medford, Oregon. Like his predecessors in the "accidental profession," Stetter had entered publishing through the back door. He began his education at the University of California at Berkeley, was drafted into the military in 1968, trained as an air traffic controller, and in 1969 went to Vietnam. After eleven months as an artillery observer on a scout helicopter, he mustered out of the army. Returning to school at California State University in Sacramento, he completed a degree in English in 1972.[37]

Newly graduated and unsure what he wanted to do next, Stetter received one of those providential telephone calls from a friend, asking if he would like to come to work in the production department of Northland Press, a subsidiary of Justin Industries located in Flagstaff, Arizona. Stetter went to Flagstaff and, with rapid staff turnover, soon found himself editor-in-chief at Northland. In 1975, he became head of publications at the prestigious Museum of Northern Arizona, which recently had expanded into publishing. Its products included regional trade books, as well as titles in archaeology and Native American and southwestern studies.[38]

Stetter met his future wife, married, and in 1981 accepted a job as editor of the Max C. Fleischmann Series in Great Basin Natural History at the University of Nevada Press (UNP). That press's director, Robert Laxalt (brother of Sen. Paul Laxalt), retired suddenly in 1983, and Stetter found himself serving as acting director and then director of the University of Nevada Press. This press focused on regional and natural history studies.

When the A&M Press director's job became available, he immediately expressed interest, in part because the character of the press reflected his own interests in regional and natural history, and in part because TAMUP and its staff had earned a "great reputation" nationally.[39] When he arrived on the Texas A&M campus, Stetter was struck by its physical size. Like Lyman, he found life in College Station formal compared with his western experiences. Stetter also sensed that Frank Wardlaw's presence still loomed large in the life and operations of the press. The new building was amazing; and, compared with many university presses, TAMUP's financial condition was strong.[40]

By training and experience, Stetter seemed a "natural" for TAMUP. He began work in September, 1988, and, in cooperation with the staff, developed a comprehensive report for the new university president, William H. Mobley. The report identified three types of books published by the Texas A&M Press: specialized books for scholars and libraries, trade books for the general public, and crossover books serving both. The white paper cautioned Mobley that scholarly books most often do not make their own way in the marketplace but rather must be subsidized both indirectly (by salary appropriations accorded the press by the university) and directly (by publication grants for individual titles and major gift endowments funding an entire series of books).[41] In the report, Stetter recalled that TAMUP had been founded with a threefold mission: (1) to promote the educational goals and enhance the prestige of Texas A&M University and its faculty; (2) to disseminate scholarship about, and preserve the heritage of, the state and region; and (3) to serve the scholarly community at large by making available important works that might not be commercially feasible. Steady expansion since the publication of the first book in 1975, he said, "has resulted in a program of some 35 books annually. In all, the press has published 282 books, of which 276 remain in print." Another 280 titles were being marketed and distributed for other regional scholarly publishers—with approximately 25 new titles being added from those sources each year.[42]

Of the 282 titles thus far published by 1989, 55 had been written by Texas A&M faculty in a wide range of disciplines, including agriculture, anthropology, archaeology, economics, engineering, geography, history, science, and veterinary medicine. Many of these books, as well as those by other regional and national authors, had received reviews in prestigious periodicals like the *New York Times Book Review*, the *Washington Post*, and the *Los*

FIG. 31. Lure of the Land: Texas County Maps and the History of Settlement *was published in cooperation with the Texas General Land Office, with the support of Commissioner Garry Mauro. By Joe B. Frantz and Mike Cox, and edited by Roger A. Griffin, this 11x17-inch book, published in 1989, presents a selection of eighty-one facsimiles of county maps held by the General Land Office. This map is of Brazos County in 1867.*

Angeles Times, as well as in business and professional journals. In 1988, TAMUP publications garnered all five of the major nonfiction awards presented annually by Texas state organizations—the Texas Institute of Letters, the Texas State Historical Association, the Daughters of the Republic of Texas, the Texas Historical Commission, and the Sons of the Republic of Texas.[43]

Stetter believed that in 1988 the press was "poised to achieve national and international prominence." Its goals would be: to continue to enhance the successful regional publication program, to stress the highest quality in those areas already under development, and to develop a new list of titles in areas in which the university desired to provide leadership in international research. Texas A&M Press books, Stetter explained, would carry the idea of genuine scholarly achievement wherever books bearing its imprint went. He projected an evolutionary growth in production over the next decade, from 35 titles annually to 50. He also announced the beginning of a new series of scholarly books on Jungian analytical psychology—"an area that is not being addressed by any other university press"—under the general editorship of an A&M faculty member, Dr. David Rosen.[44]

Stetter described the organization of the press, delineating the role and function of each department. He discussed the membership and functions of the Faculty Advisory Committee and the press's Advisory Council, and briefly described the financial management of the press, noting the nature of the capital accounts and the source and content of the revolving series accounts.[45]

This report was comprehensive and carefully considered. It recalled Frank Wardlaw's initial report, "The Beginning," addressed to President Jack K. Williams in September, 1974. In a similar fashion, it professed to mark the beginning of an auspicious new era in the affairs of Texas A&M University Press.

Stetter began his work by dividing the editorial department into two distinct functions, giving Noel Parsons responsibility for acquisitions and the new title of editor-in-chief. Mary Lenn Dixon would take responsibility for copyediting. But university problems soon would intrude upon TAMUP operations.

The press was not alone in experiencing changes. When Stetter arrived on campus, the university's administration was in a state of flux. Arthur Hansen, who had served as chancellor of the A&M system since 1982, had resigned in January, 1986, and had been replaced by Perry Lee Adkisson. William H. Mobley had replaced Frank Vandiver as university president in September, 1988. In August, 1991, Herbert H. Richardson would assume the chancellor's chair when Adkisson returned to teaching. These changes in the top administrative posts at both the university and system levels mattered to the press, which reported directly to the president. Financial pressures upon the university were mounting, creating uncertainty for the press. As on other campuses, questions were raised about the university funds appropriated for the press and whether the press could be required to become financially self-sufficient. In other areas—for example, at the bookstore and in food services—efforts were being made to privatize operations in order to remove these entities from university funding. In time, some of the efforts at privatization and reorganization made the university subject to audits, investigations, charges, and general dissension. None of this, of course, was anticipated when Stetter assumed the reins of TAMUP.

Neither could Stetter anticipate that, only seven months after being made director of the press, he would become a candidate for emergency heart surgery. While the procedure was successful, the surgery and the illness and rehabilitation associated with it interfered with realization of Stetter's plans for the press—as did the unsettled state of campus affairs. Eventually, in the context of the broader university disruptions, TAMUP staff managers saw a need to take more active roles in the functioning of the press. With Stetter's approval, the staff formed an Executive Committee, which served as a management body while reporting to the director. The division heads who composed the committee were Jim Billingsley and later Susan Pettey (design and production manager), Gayla Christiansen (marketing manager), Mary Lenn Dixon (managing editor), Dianna Hein (business manager), and Noel Parsons (editor-in-chief). Hein was asked to provide information about financial operations to the department heads. Previously, financial information had gone directly to the director. The Executive Committee also was empowered to set goals, plan future programs, and help the press seek additional external funding.[46]

Despite the problems, the press continued to grow. Its growth involved change in the style and character of the books it published. The booklist for spring of 1989 included numerous books about the natural world and about women. *Baja Journey,* by Robin Carey, traced the "reveries of a sea-kayaker." *No Woman Tenderfoot,* by Harriet Kofalk, was the story of Florence Merriam Bailey, a bird-watcher, backpacker, and naturalist. *Connie Hagar,* a biography by Karen Harden McCracken, recounted the life history of a Texas bird-watcher. Lawrence Kilham's *The American Crow and the Common Raven* was the tenth in the W. L. Moody, Jr., Natural History Series. Kilham was a fellow of the American Ornithologists' Union, a professor emeritus of microbiology at Dartmouth Medical School, and a distinguished virologist. *Ronald Reagan and the Public Lands: America's Conservation Debate, 1979–1984,* by C. Brant Short, reflected the broadening of focus from the Old West to issues affecting the West today.[47]

The Old West was not forgotten in the new lists, however. Paula Mitchell Marks's *Turn Your Eyes Toward Texas* dealt with Texas pioneers Sam and Mary Maverick. Ben E. Pingenot's contribution, *Siringo,* was the biography of Charles A. Siringo, born in Texas in 1855, who became a rancher, writer, Pinkerton agent, and later a freelance detective. "Texas and wildcatters—they go together," said Patillo Higgins in Robert W. McDaniel's *Patillo Higgins and the Search for Texas Oil,* a work which combined the essence of the Old West and modern oil entrepreneurship.[48]

One Woman's Army: A Black Officer Remembers the WAC (Women's Air Corps), by Charity Adams Earley; and *Safe at Home: A Baseball Wife's Story,* by Sharon Hargrove and Richard Hauer Costa, rounded out the substantial list of books about women published by TAMUP in the spring of 1989.[49]

Diana Lee Vance had been on the staff several months by that spring. She provided clerical assistance to the editors, to marketing, and to any other department that needed it. Vance took the job with the understanding that she could work full-time while taking a part-time course load at A&M in order to complete her degree in psychology. A self-described "book-aholic," Vance was particularly struck by the diversity of authors, faculty, and staff she encountered in the world of publishing.[50]

Joyce Smith also joined the staff that spring as receptionist and secretary to the director. Smith extended a warm, friendly greeting to all who crossed the TAMUP threshold. Unfortunately, her time at the press was cut short. She died following a brief, serious illness in 1994. The staff dedicated the garden at the building's entry to her memory.[51]

The emphasis on women, the military, and natural history continued. Anne Noggle's *For God, Country, and the Thrill of It: Women Air Force Service Pilots in World War II,* the first title in the Charles and Elizabeth Prothro Texas Photography Series, appeared in the spring of 1990. *The Nature of Texas: A Feast of Native Beauty from Texas Highways Magazine,* edited by nature writer Howard Peacock and the eleventh title in the Louise Lindsey Merrick Natural Environment Series, also was issued then. So was *The Bats of Texas,* by David J.

Schmidly (a longtime member of the TAMUP Faculty Advisory Committee). If you were "curious about a day in the life of a prairie dog, the engineering skills of the beaver, or why the armadillo wears armor," Ilo Hiller's *Introducing Mammals to Young Naturalists* was the book to read.[52] TAMUP was enhancing its traditional Texas base and regional identity, while at the same time raising its scholarly profile.

Elizabeth Silverthorne contributed a second book to the Clayton Wheat Williams Texas Life Series, the popular and unusual study entitled *Christmas in Texas,* which was released in 1990 (and reprinted in 1993 and 1994) as the third volume in the series. This work underscored the rich diversity of Texas life and culture, encompassing African, Czech, English, German, Mexican, Polish, Wendish, Yugoslavian, and other traditions. Silverthorne wrote two other books for TAMUP series as well: *Legends and Lore of Texas Wildflowers* (Louise Lindsey Merrick Natural Environment Series, Number 24) and *Women Pioneers in Texas Medicine,* written with Geneve Fulgham (Centennial Series of the Association of Former Students, Number 70).

One of the most interesting projects had to do with the publication in 1990 of the first volume of a five-volume history of the Texas Senate. The work came about, as then Lt. Gov. Bill Hobby said, because a newly elected senator, Chet Edwards, asked him where he could find a history of the Texas Senate. None existed, and "we decided to remedy that situation." Betty King, secretary of the Texas Senate, and Patsy Spaw, engrossing and enrolling clerk, assumed the formidable task of writing the history as a multivolume set. With her staff, Spaw produced a remarkable first volume, which traces the history of Texas through the work of the Texas Senate from the days of the Texas Republic to the Civil War. Stetter, who had a personal interest in book design and composition, decided that the press should also publish a limited edition of the volumes, in a special slipcase, which would be signed by the lieutenant governor. The books, in both formats, were well received. Lieutenant Governor Hobby and university President Bill Mobley, Stetter recalled, were particularly pleased.[53]

The pace of publishing quickened. In the fall of 1991, the press introduced a new series, Studies in Architecture and Culture, sponsored by the Center for the Advancement of Studies in Architecture (CASA) and edited by Malcolm Quantrill, Distinguished Professor of Architecture at Texas A&M University. The first volume, *Constancy and Change in Architecture,* edited by Quantrill and Bruce J. Webb, a member of the architecture faculty at the University of Houston, offered studies of contemporary problems and conflicts in the philosophy and methodology of architectural practice, written by leading international architects. Over the next few years, Quantrill and other architects addressed *Urban Forms, Suburban Dreams; Modernity and Its Other: A Postscript to Contemporary Architecture;* and *Culture of Silence: Architecture's Fifth Dimension.*[54]

The Lighthouses of Texas, by T. Lindsay Baker, illuminated the literary landscape in 1991, as did a photographic study of the German Hill County of Texas and a fascinating autobiography by Hallie Crawford Stillwell, *I'll Gather My Geese.* In April, 1990, *Texas Monthly* magazine termed Stillwell "arguably the most famous rancher in West Texas." A history of veterinary medicine in Texas by Henry C. Dethloff and Donald H. Dyal examined the profession that works at the interface of the human-animal bond—a bond that marked humankind's first step toward civilization and only grew stronger over time. The twelfth publication issued in TAMUP's acclaimed Environmental History Series was a book about detergents: *Biodegradable,* by William McGucken.[55]

The list continued to grow in length, quality, and diversity. Over the next few years, publications ranged from a study of a Spanish governor of Texas, Manuel Salcedo, who governed from 1808 to 1813, to a very contemporary political study of the quest for the American presidency. Perhaps one of the most unusual books was *The Birds of Tikal: An Annotated Checklist for Tikal National Park and Petén, Guatemala,* by Randell A. Beavers. Liz Carpenter, prominent in Texas letters, authored *Getting Better All the Time* and *Ruffles and Flourishes,* both published in 1993. That same year, two Texas A&M professors of philosophy, Robert W. Burch and Herman J. Saatkamp, produced the first installment of their multivolume *Frontiers in American Philosophy.*[56] The press, somewhat like the university, in the space of almost two decades had developed in-house traditions and dynamics that helped to sustain a flow of good books. In the summer of 1994, to help continue this flow, John R. Hill, Jr., and Peggy Sloan Hill pledged a part of a trust to the press to support its publishing program.

Complications arose, however, due in part to Stetter's past illness and personal problems and in part to the unsettled state of the university administration. In 1993, financial and management reviews of TAMUP operations identified a number of staff, morale, and fiscal problems. In the fall of 1993, Stetter resigned as director of the Texas A&M University Press and accepted a similar position at the University of Southern Illinois.[57]

When problems became apparent in the internal management of the press, President Mobley (to whom the press director reported) assigned Mary Miller, the university's director of operational analysis, to give Stetter special assistance and management advice. Then, when Stetter resigned from the press, he recommended to Mobley that Miller be appointed interim director. Miller recalls that, during an A&M Mothers' Club coffee, she and President Mobley, together with Richard Smith and other administrators, were discussing the appointment of an interim press director. Mobley turned to her and asked, "What do you know about publishing?"

"I read books," she replied.

"That will do," he said.

It would not, of course, be enough for a permanent director, but Miller's expertise certainly was what was needed at the time, and in October, 1993, Mobley appointed her interim director of the Texas A&M University Press.[58]

Born into a military family living in Key West, Florida, during World War II and raised in New Orleans, Louisiana, Miller graduated from New Orleans's Loyola University with a degree in psychology. After marrying Richard Miller, a chemist, she moved with her husband from Princeton University to Michigan State University. In Michigan, she began a career in social work, progressing from that into a state project on management development focused on state income maintenance and child welfare programs. Miller became a specialist in management techniques and strategic planning. Eventually the family relocated to Atlanta, where she began work as an independent management consultant.[59]

In 1986, having moved to Texas A&M University and following a few years devoted to raising a family, Miller accepted the position of director of operational analysis under Vice President for Finance and Administration Robert Smith. Miller knew and understood people, budgeting, and management; and she plunged into her work energetically.[60] Meanwhile, the university administration continued to change. That same summer, the Board of Regents promoted Mobley to the chancellor's position, replacing Chancellor Herbert H. Richardson, and appointed an interim president, E. Dean Gage, a doctor of veterinary medicine who was a pioneer in spinal and neu-

FIG. 32. *Artist Herb Booth is widely known for his drawings and paintings of wildlife and sporting scenes. The press published* In the Sporting Tradition *in the Joe and Betty Moore Texas Art Series, with an introduction by Michael McIntosh and a foreword by Meredith Long, in 1993.*

ral surgery and a former associate dean of A&M's College of Veterinary Medicine.

When Miller moved to her new office at TAMUP, she found an unexpected degree of pain among the press staff. Morale and enthusiasm, as well as communication among staff members, were in decline, and the staff felt frustrated. To Miller, however, it was clear that all the staff members were tremendously talented and dedicated. They loved the press and their work. They maintained positive relationships with authors and retained a strong base of support among traditional friends and patrons of the press.[61]

Miller's approach primarily focused on restoring communication and self-confidence and rebuilding the team. Staff members were asked to leave their office doors open, and problems were to be resolved by one-on-one communication. Regular and frequent (often biweekly) staff meetings were held at which *all* topics were discussed. This meant that each department and each staff member talked about his or her own work and problems, and the others' work and problems. Miller held a retreat, treated the staff to management training sessions, tried to restore a sense of fun in the workplace, and challenged staff members to take risks and exceed their own expectations of themselves. Miller also set the entire staff to work creating a new strategic plan. A year and five months passed. The atmosphere and the work environment improved dramatically.[62]

Karol Murrah, a 1994 A&M journalism graduate who began an internship at the press in January, 1994, recalls that, if there were personnel problems when she arrived, they were not noticeable. Although she never really had been aware of TAMUP during her undergraduate days (most students probably were unaware of the press's existence), she always had liked books and writing. After completing her internship and her degree, Murrah remained with the press to work full-time in marketing, and when an assistant editor position opened in July, 1995, she readily applied and was hired. Like the rest of the staff, she quickly became engrossed in the business of making books.[63]

In April, 1994, the Board of Regents appointed Dr. Ray M. Bowen, a 1958 graduate of Texas A&M University and a mechanical engineer, as university president, replacing the interim president, Gage. In July, the regents named Barry Thompson—a former president of both Tarleton State University and West Texas State University, who held a doctorate in education from Texas A&M University—as the new chancellor of the Texas A&M University System, replacing Mobley. Things began to settle down, and the time came to select a permanent director for TAMUP. A search committee appointed by President Bowen and headed by Fred Heath, director of the Texas A&M University Libraries, who was assisted by Miller, cast a net far and wide.

Miller recalled that part of the "net" was the Internet, denoting the onset of the Digital Age, which heralded such marked changes in the book industry. As the search for a new TAMUP director began, university press staff and personnel across the nation were expressing, via the Internet, grave concern about the welfare and status of university presses. Some were ceasing operations, while others were losing funding and support from their universities. Most were experiencing declines in sales or structural changes in their marketing programs, as more and more sales went to large bookstore

FIG. 33. *The press has published several popular books about Texas A&M University, the campus, and its traditions. From the 1994 publishing season came Donald B. and Mary Jo Powell's book* The Fightin' Texas Aggie Band. *As number 53 in the Centennial Series of the Association of Former Students, it shows the value and importance of that series to the press's overall publishing program.*

chains that demanded greater discounts and returned massive quantities of unsold books at the end of the marketing season. Mom-and-pop bookstores and university and public library sales, which had been the mainstay of university and regional publishers, were in decline. Moreover, people were asking a very basic question: what form would books take in an increasingly electronic environment? Now manuscripts conceivably could go from inception to publication and never leave the electronic media. Would the electronic media one day replace the printed media? What role would the Internet play in bookmaking and book marketing?[64]

Miller released an item on the Internet that contradicted the gloom and doom rampant in academic press circles. She invited applications for the directorship of the Texas A&M University Press—a press, she explained, that enjoyed the support of the university's administration, faculty, and former students. The A&M Press had a strong regional booklist, an impressive number of award-winning scholarly books, one of the finest press buildings in the United States, and an exceptionally healthy financial condition. Who could ignore the opportunity to head such a viable university press?[65]

Chapter 5

STRATEGIC PLANNING

Thomas M. Rotell, director of the prestigious University of Pennsylvania Press, might have thought that he could ignore an e-mail invitation to apply for a comparable position at a press less known, less mature, and still growing. But the message from Mary Miller stirred and intrigued him, as did the challenge of becoming a part of a healthy, young university press that already had an interesting history and a respectable position within the industry. Rotell submitted a letter of application, thinking that he would at least satisfy his curiosity. When he found himself on the search committee's list of finalists for the position, he still was uncommitted but felt obligated to go to College Station for an interview. That interview, the magnetism of the Southwest and its literature, and the obvious support proffered by the university convinced him that he should indeed come to Texas A&M University to direct its press.[1]

A coal miner's son—and a coal miner's grandson—from Scranton, Pennsylvania, Rotell had been born at the height of the Great Depression. His father was determined that his son would have the education he himself had been denied. Rotell was the first of his family to go to college. He completed an undergraduate degree in biology at Pennsylvania State University, thinking he wanted to work toward a Ph.D. in that subject in order to teach at the university level. With that in mind, Rotell began graduate work in biology at Ohio State University, taught a laboratory course, married, and discovered that he really did not particularly care for research and teaching. When a friend who was a salesman with Macmillan Publishing Company suggested he consider a career in publishing, Rotell was interested.[2]

While most in the field may enter publishing accidentally, one common tie is that they like books. Rotell was no exception. He accepted a job with Macmillan as a sales representative based in Michigan, with marketing responsibilities for Michigan, Ohio, and Pennsylvania. In a short time, Rotell was promoted to acquisitions editor, with offices in New York. Then he became acquisitions editor for biology in Macmillan's College Division.[3]

Rotell remembers that, in browsing through the correspondence and records of some of his predecessors, he came across the files of James Michener, who had published his first book, *Tales of the South Pacific*, while working for Macmillan. After ten years, Rotell left Macmillan to become editorial director and then director of marketing at Random House.[4]

With friends in the world of scholarly publishing and after having spent about twenty years in commercial publishing, Rotell decided to take the somewhat uncommon step of moving into university press publishing. In 1978, he became director of Teachers College Press at Columbia University, which specialized in a wide range of educational materials, from scholarly monographs to public school educational texts and testing materials. In a university setting, Rotell believed, one could publish the books one believed in, with profit being less of a motive (although income always would be a concern) and in an excellent work environment. In 1983, he left Columbia for the University of Pennsylvania Press. The scholarly list at Pennsylvania was much larger and more diverse, and the press had a prestigious backlist. Over the next twelve years, under Rotell's direction, the University of Pennsylvania Press further expanded its booklists and enhanced its size, reputation, and prestige. The Pennsylvania Press and its university, already strong, grew even stronger.[5]

Why did Rotell decide to leave this near-perfect situation in the world of academic publishing to go to College Station? Rotell heard this question from many friends, authors, and University of Pennsylvania administrators. While no single response would have been accurate, several elements contributed to Rotell's moving to Texas A&M. Mary Miller's e-mail, a letter from Fred Heath, and an interview with an obviously interested and enthusiastic search committee and administration all figured in the decision. The people he met—administrators, faculty, and press staff—almost universally were "concerned, interested, positive, motivated, and enthusiastic," Rotell said. TAMUP was in good financial condition, far better than most university presses. It had tremendous support. Its traditions and work ethic were well established. It had the "psychological, emotional, and financial support" to make a truly great university press.[6] In a word, it was an opportunity too good to pass up. As his predecessors Frank Wardlaw and Lloyd Lyman had discovered, it was very difficult to say no to Texas A&M.

When Rotell arrived in March of 1995, he had reasonably simple and straightforward goals. He wanted to enhance the reputation of both the press and the university, and he wanted to do so in a financially responsible way.[7] He began his work by seeking to build within the staff a new consensus—a spirit of cooperation and a commitment to the tasks that lay ahead. What were those tasks to be? What kind of publisher did the Texas A&M University Press want to be? Employing a management style similar to Mary Miller's, Rotell sought to build a future to which all at the press could be committed. Rotell felt strongly that TAMUP should focus more actively on scholarly publications—particularly on those with an international aspect—and he wanted to make sure that the staff agreed. Through biweekly staff meetings, individual conferences, and formal and informal discussions, he found that the staff indeed concurred.[8]

A plan emerged that would set the A&M Press on a new course, albeit one conditioned by past experiences and achievements. TAMUP would retain and strengthen its traditional position in the Texas, southwestern, and military subject areas. It would seek to expand those areas where it already had a presence—architecture, Borderlands studies, Eastern European studies, natural history, and nautical archaeology. It also would move strongly into selected new publishing areas. One of these was presidential studies, an area invited by the scheduled opening of the George Bush Presidential Library on the Texas A&M University campus in the fall of 1997 and the establishment of the George Bush School of Government and Public Service, including a Center for Presidential Studies and a Center for Public Leadership Studies.[9]

The development of several book series in presidential studies was presaged in 1994 by the publication of *The Quest for the Presidency, 1992*. This tome, authored by *Newsweek* writers Peter Goldman, Thomas M. DeFrank, Mark Miller, Andrew Murr, and Tom Matthews, examined the elections that brought Bill Clinton to the White House. That same year, the press initiated work on a Presidential Rhetoric Series that resulted in the 1996 publication of *Beyond the Rhetorical Presidency,* edited by Martin J. Medhurst, a professor of speech communication and the coordinator of the university's new Program in Presidential Rhetoric. The announcement of the new book title and the series explained that "Theodore Roosevelt and Woodrow Wilson in particular wrought profound changes in the American presidency. Chief among those was the use of rhetoric—the capacity to use symbols in a persuasive way. It was a radical departure and the start of an evolution toward direct appeals from the president to the general public."

In 1995, TAMUP took a significant step toward establishment of a series in general presidential studies. Joseph V. Hughes, Jr. (a 1975 graduate of Texas A&M and president of Spindletop Exploration Company), and his wife, Holly Oldfield Hughes, of Midland, made an unrestricted gift of $50,000 to the press, which was used to endow a new Series in the Presidency and Leadership Studies. Efforts by retired Chancellor Frank W. Hubert initiated this donation. For years, Joe Hughes had hunted with Hubert and had spent many nights in Hubert's deer camp, whose chief adornment was a collection of books published by TAMUP. Hughes enjoyed these books. In later years, when he mentioned that he would like to do something for A&M but was not sure in what area, Hubert reminded him of his interest in the TAMUP books. The Hughes gift, placed in a revolving fund account, marked the inception of a significant new publication direction.[10]

Presidential scholar James P. Pfiffner of George Mason University in Virginia agreed to serve as series editor. A distinguished group of eight national scholars, including two members of the Texas A&M faculty—H. W. Brands of the history department and George C. Edwards III of the political science department—were named to the series's editorial advisory board. "The series focuses on individual presidencies, how they have been structured and how individual presidents have related to Congress and the Supreme Court," TAMUP editor Mary Lenn Dixon explained. The series also maintains close ties with scholarship emanating from the Bush Library.[11]

The series advisory committee and the press soon issued the first title in the series, a revision of an already classic study by Louis Fisher, *The Politics of Shared Power: Congress and the Executive,* which had been published first in 1981. The book, which appeared in both cloth and paper in the spring of 1998, kicked off the series with a "very high profile book and author." By the fall of 1998, TAMUP had three other books in production and a considerable list of titles under contract for future publication in the series. These books in the making included a study of how Congress and the executive office share power, an analysis of the presidency and environmental issues, an examination of the presidential exercise of military power, a book about national security strategies, and a review of the Bush presidency.[12]

The Eastern European Series, under the general editorship of Stjepan G. Mestrovic, a professor of sociology at Texas A&M University, focused on the post–Cold War political and military life of Eastern Europe. The first title, Norman Cigar's *Genocide in Bosnia: The Policy of "Ethnic Cleansing"* (1995), was followed in 1996 by Philip J. Cohen's *Serbia's Secret War: Propaganda and the Deceit of History* (in both cloth and paper). Next came *The New Georgia: Space, Society, Politics* (1996), in which Revaz Gachechiladze provided an inside view of the great changes (and lack of changes) within the former Soviet satellite. TAMUP published three new titles in the series in 1997, and the paperback edition of Cohen's *Serbia's Secret War* was reprinted. New books included Frederick Quinn's *Democracy at Dawn,* which examined the sweeping democratic reforms affecting Poland and other former Communist bloc countries; and Meštrović's edited collection, *The Conceit of Innocence: Losing the Conscience of the West in the War Against Bosnia,* which lifted the curtain on Western moral and foreign policy dilemmas resulting from the breakup of the Soviet Union. *The Political Analysis of Postcommunism,* the first American edition of a 1995 study of the Ukraine by Volodymyr Polokhalo, editor-in-chief of the Ukrainian journal *Political Thought,* was written to enlighten Westerners about the traumatic changes experienced by a society converting from Communism.[13] In 1998, Csaba Teglas's *Budapest Exit: A Memoir of Fascism, Communism, and Freedom* became the seventh title in the Eastern European Series.

Karol Murrah, who joined the editorial deparment in July, 1995, when the press was on the brink of expansion, noted that the various presidential series, the Eastern European Series, and the growing list of trade and crossover books (titles appealing to both academic and general readers) were making Texas A&M University Press more widely known throughout the United States.[14]

Natural history, a TAMUP staple since the press's inception, continued to provide important entries. In the fall of 1995, three new titles in natural history appeared. The first, *Lone Star Dinosaurs,* was authored by Louis Jacobs, director of the Shuler Museum of Paleontology and professor of geological sciences at Southern Methodist University in Dallas. With color plates, photos, and line drawings by Karen Carr, the book told "for the first time the exciting stories of the giant beasts that once roamed where jumbo jets now roll down runways at DFW Airport and where hikers make camp in Big Bend." The volume was picturesque, informative, fun, exciting, and geared to general audiences young and old, but it also was scholarly.[15]

Also published in 1995, Eric R. Swanson's *Geo-Texas: A Guide to the Earth Sciences* brought together astronomy, geology, meteorology, oceanography, and environmental studies in a unique guide to Texas' multifaceted environment. An intriguing and controversial study of birds by Alexander F. Skutch, an internationally renowned ornithologist, expounded the author's belief that "birds' mental capacities have been grossly underestimated." It was published in the Louise Lindsey Merrick Natural Environment Series.[16]

The nine military history titles produced in the fall of 1995 ran the gamut of American warfare from the Revolution to the post-Vietnam era. Among these were *Rebel Brothers: The Civil War Letters of the Truehearts,* edited by Edward B. Williams; *Fallen Guidon: The Saga of Confederate General Jo Shelby's March to Mexico,* by Edwin Adams Davis; Frederick Zeh's *An Immigrant Soldier in the Mexican War;* Edward G. Miller's *A Dark and Bloody Ground: The Hürtgen Forest and the Roer River Dams, 1944–1945; The Texas Military Experience: From the Revolution through World War II,* edited by Joseph G. Dawson III; a Vietnam War tragedy, *Sappers in the Wire: The Life and Death of Firebase Mary Ann,* by Keith William Nolan; Edward P. Metzner's *More than a Soldier's War: Pacification in Vietnam; A Very Short War: The Mayagüez and the Battle of Koh Tang,* by John G. Guilmartin, Jr., the story of a post–Vietnam War encounter off the Cambodian coast; and a paperback reprint of William H. Bartsch's *Doomed at the Start: American Pursuit Pilots in the Philippines, 1941–1942,* which the press originally had published in 1992.[17]

During 1996, the staff continued to work on defining TAMUP's goals and ambitions. Interesting and unusual books were released. One was *Bigmama Didn't Shop at Woolworth's,* by Sunny Nash, a black writer's account of growing up in segregated Texas in the 1950s. Also published were a biography of the first Mexican-American federal judge, *All Rise: Reynaldo G. Garza, the First Federal Mexican-American Judge,* by Louise Ann Fisch; a regional study of Indians caught between converging empires, *The Caddos, the Wichitas, and the United States, 1846–1901,* by F. Todd Smith; and a bevy of books on Texas topics ranging from wanderlust to women to wildflowers.

In the spring of 1996 the C. A. Brannen Series, established by J. P. Brannen and Frances Brannen Vick in honor of their father who attended Texas A&M and served with distinction in World War I, was officially launched with the publication of their father's memoir, *Over There: A Marine in the Great War.*

Also in 1996, TAMUP initiated a Studies in Nautical Archaeology series that would offer brief, topical studies to complement the larger site reports of the early Nautical Archaeology Series. The first three titles were *Those Vulgar Tubes: External Sanitary Accommodations Aboard European Ships of the Fifteenth Through Seventeenth Centuries,* by Joe J. Simmons III; *Ships' Bilge Pumps: A History of Their Development, 1500–1900,* by Thomas J. Oertling; and *The Development of the Rudder: A Technological Tale,* by Lawrence V. Mott.

In natural history, the press published a revised edition of *Javelinas and Other Peccaries: Their Biology, Management, and Use,* by Lyle K. Sowls (originally published by the University of Arizona Press in 1984).[18]

At a meeting of the Advisory Council in November, 1996, Chancellor Barry Thompson announced the establishment of a Texas A&M University System Matching Funds Program to encourage publications by scholars at Texas A&M's associated campuses away from College Station. For each of two books annually for two years, the system would match a $2,500 publishing subvention provided by the associated campus (giving the press a total of $5,000 per title). Four campuses agreed to participate: West Texas A&M University (which previously had entered into a similar agreement with TAMUP), Texas A&M University at Texarkana, Texas A&M University at Commerce, and Texas A&M University at Kingsville. As noted earlier, Tarleton State University had entered into a publishing agreement with the press when Thompson was president of that institution, and West Texas A&M had instituted a similar arrangement while Thompson was president there. Now Chancellor Thompson extended the liaison to other universities within the A&M System.[19]

At the same meeting, TAMUP director Rotell informed the Advisory Council that the press had scheduled a substantial increase in the number of titles to be produced during the 1996–97 academic year. He also announced the establishment of a new book series, the Texas A&M Anthropology Series, under the general editorship of anthropology professor D. Gentry Steele. The Anthropology Series utilized an advisory committee representing universities across the nation. The committee included William Irons, professor of biocultural anthropology at Northwestern University; Conrad Kotak, professor of cultural anthropology at the University of Michigan; James F. O'Connel, professor of ethnoarchaeology and cultural anthropology at the University of Utah; Harry J. Shafer, professor of archaeology at Texas A&M University; Eric Trinkaus, professor of biological anthropology at the University of New Mexico; Michael R. Waters, associate professor of geoarchaeology at Texas A&M University; and Patty Jo Watson, professor of archaeology at Washington University.[20]

The first volume in the new anthropology series, a copublication with the British Museum, was an intriguing study of the "new science" of recreating in clay the visages of humans who had lived long ago. *Making Faces: Using Forensic and Archaeological Evidence,* by John Prag and Richard Neave, describes the detective work that made it possible to recreate in clay the faces of such famous figures as King Midas, Philip of Macedon, and "Lindow Man."[21]

While TAMUP was expanding and its future was looking bright indeed, some dark clouds were visible on the horizon of the larger world of scholarly publishing. As Rotell explained, "The scholarly monograph was under serious duress. Every press has seen sales [of individual volumes] decline dramatically." Libraries were spending more of their budgets on technology and computer hardware and software than on books. Book orders were declining. Declining budgets faced government programs that formerly had supported or in other ways encouraged publication. In contrast to earlier projections, post–Cold War trends were diminishing, rather than increasing, federal funding for the sciences and education. As if to underscore the serious implications for university presses, Rice University announced that its press, a member of the TAMUP distribution consortium, would cease operations in December, 1996. TAMUP purchased a large part of Rice's book inventory and took over publication of a number of its titles, beginning in 1997.[22]

In a similar vein, Maureen Creamer, the press's publicity and advertising manager, who had joined the staff in 1985, sensed that, even within the past decade, the marketing of university press books had changed significantly. Born in Saint Louis, Missouri, Creamer had spent most of her early years in Houston. She began studying journalism at the University of Texas at Austin, but, she explained laconically, after a class assignment to visit and prepare news releases about the city jails, she decided to change her major to English. Her senior year, Creamer was associate editor of the University of Texas annual, *The Longhorn.* It was a prodigious yearbook and an exacting job that demanded unusual editorial and managerial skills. That, and a brief experience after graduation as a technical editor in Houston, made her want to be in the publishing business.[23]

As part of the press's marketing department, Creamer had to cope with continual change. Who were the current buyers of university press books, and particularly buyers of the sorts of books published by TAMUP? They included A&M students and former students, A&M faculty, faculty of other national and international institutions (who had to be reached by direct mail and strategically placed ads), and the general public. For the last group, publicity and promotion were increasingly critical. The book consumer, regardless of category, Creamer noted, was aging. Younger readers increasingly had turned away from paper to the electronic media. Even at TAMUP, some of the younger staff and student interns were as interested in creating web pages and posting information about books on the Internet as they were in the technical processes involved in producing a traditional printed book.[24]

What did this mean for the future of university press publishing? Already it meant greater competition in a declining market, the necessity for innovation, and constant attention to the mix of books published in academic, trade, and crossover markets.

While TAMUP remained in relatively strong financial condition, increasingly it—like other university presses—found itself on the horns of a dilemma. How could it continue to publish less and less profitable scholarly books, in keeping with its commitment to the academic community, and in so doing continue to weaken its financial position? Should it bolster its financial position by publishing more books geared to general audiences (these generate more income)? In so doing, it would almost certainly arouse disdain and displeasure in the academic community, which would feel its needs were being served less well. Wolves howled on both sides of the door—financial wolves on one side, academic wolves on the other. The trick was to be financially responsible while publishing effectively, and this could be achieved only by constantly refining and monitoring the press's policies, programs, and procedures.[25]

The solution, Rotell believed, was to continue publishing a variety of titles, to focus on existing areas where the press possessed strength and presence, to build new bridges in those areas where the university clearly was prominent but which were not reflected in current TAMUP lists, and to withdraw from areas best served by other university presses. Specifically, this meant continuing to expand in Texas and southwestern regional studies, in Eastern European studies, in military history, natural science, natural history, and nautical archaeology. It also meant venturing prominently into the field of presidential studies; building titles in the neglected areas of Borderlands studies and architecture; and creating new series and publishing programs in agriculture and veterinary medicine—fields in which Texas A&M University traditionally had been highly esteemed.[26]

Effective publishing also meant enhancing the functional systems related to the press and maximizing their effectiveness. The Faculty Advisory Committee, for example, could be selected more carefully to reflect current publishing emphases. More staff input could improve decisions regarding costs, prices, and print run (the number of copies of a title to be printed). Similarly, reprint decisions could be weighed more carefully and enhanced by greater staff consideration and input.[27]

Subsidiary rights—reprint permissions, as well as film, media, and especially international rights, given the expanding role of the university and the increasingly international focus of TAMUP publications—needed more careful attention. Traditionally a sideline in university publishing, international rights promised to produce an increasingly significant portion of the press's income. To address the needs in this area, Rotell directed his assistant, Linda Salitros, to assume responsibility for domestic and international rights, while book club rights continued to be managed by Gayla Christiansen, the marketing manager. This was one part of the fine-tuning process Rotell had envisioned.[28]

Making books was both an art and, of necessity, a business. The press needed to distribute books more efficiently, collect more expeditiously, and, in the process, keep more exact electronic records so as to monitor progress. Order fulfillment and financial management needed to be adjusted and an accrual accounting system adopted. Rotell and Christiansen assumed more responsibility for expanding distribution. Part of this expansion reflected the addition of two new members to the Texas A&M University Press Consortium: a small new regional press, Winedale Publishing of Houston, Texas; and a significant new client, the *Dallas Morning News,* in its capacity as publisher of the redoubtable *Texas Almanac.* Winedale Publishing was founded in 1996 to publish literary fiction and quality nonfiction; its inaugural work was Leon Hale's *Home Spun.* In 1997, Christiansen and Rotell completed agreements with the *Dallas Morning News* for TAMUP to serve as exclusive distributor of the *Texas Almanac,* then in its fifty-ninth edition.[29] This marked a significant expansion in the evolution of the press as a regional book distributor. Distribution arrangements with Baylor University Press, the Texas Review Press, and McWhiney Foundation Press (a publisher of Civil War titles) further strengthened the consortium's presence.

In the spring of 1997, following a year of study and reappraisal, a new strategic plan was adopted, articulating the course of Texas A&M University Press's future development:

> *The primary mission of the press is to help the University achieve its paramount purposes of teaching, research, dissemination of scholarly inquiry, and public service by publishing books and electronic products that meet or exceed the highest industry standards. The Press will accomplish this goal and enhance the reputation of the University regionally, nationally, and internationally by pursuing the following strategies and tactics:*
>
> - *to maintain and enhance publication of trade and scholarly books, and vigorously expand publishing efforts into textbooks, reference books, professional books, and electronics.*
> - *publishing more products in established series (Nautical Archaeology, Eastern European Studies, Architecture and Culture, Natural History, and Military History), while firmly establishing new series in such areas as Borderlands studies, presidential studies, anthropology, agriculture, and veterinary medicine.*[30]

In addition, the press proposed actively to publish timely, topical, and substantive books that intelligently reflected the latest research and opinion of Texas A&M University scholars on issues of great importance to the general public. The press would focus on a smaller number of promising fields, while phasing out those fields where it was less competitive academically and financially. It would seek to publish more scholarly works that attracted wider audiences and that would contribute to breaking down "artificial barriers between academic disciplines and lead to new syntheses of knowledge and learning."[31]

Finally, the press would aggressively pursue the sale of foreign rights to its publications, actively seek endowment funds and publication subsidies, and further develop and extend its funding and publishing agreements with other Texas A&M System campuses, while improving all its functional operations, qualitatively and quantitatively. The new strategic plan also pledged continuing effort to create "a working environment at the Press that is exciting, challenging, humane, fair minded, and results oriented."[32] If the past were any indication, TAMUP's future promised to be both challenging and exciting.

The 1997 book list confirmed the promise. Frank E. Vandiver, president emeritus of Texas A&M University, produced another of his epochal military studies, *Shadows of Vietnam: Lyndon Johnson's Wars.* The result of eight years of thought, research, and writing, this was the masterwork of a biographer who had honed his skills on subjects as varied as Stonewall Jackson and John J. Pershing. When John and Sara Lindsey hosted the publication party in their Houston home in July, the excitement was palpable.[33]

In the fall of 1997, anticipating the November opening of the Bush Presidential Library, TAMUP released *George Herbert Walker Bush: A Photographic Profile,* compiled by David Valdez. As Bush's personal photographer during his second term as vice president and his four years as president, Valdez had his camera's eye trained on history. The book documented such historic moments as elections, inaugurations, and the tearing down of the Berlin Wall, as well as the rarer and more personal moments of a president at work, rest, and play. After leaving the White House, Valdez had become general manager of photography for Walt Disney World Company in Orlando, Florida.[34]

While titles scheduled for 1998 would continue to carry the press into new dimensions of scholarly publishing, a strong commitment to regional publications persisted. Frank Wardlaw would have been pleased. David La Vere's *Life Among the Texas Indians: The WPA Narratives* recalled the press's very first publication, *Storms Brewed in Other Men's World,* the story of the Spanish conquest of Native American societies. Scott Cook's *Mexican Brick Culture in the Building of Texas, 1800s–1980s* also complemented the press's original focus on southwestern culture and history.

FIG. 34. *One of the press's favorite authors, Frank Vandiver, was once again on the press's list in 1997 with the publication of his nationally acclaimed* Shadows of Vietnam: Lyndon Johnson's Wars.

Further solidifying the press's commitment to natural history were *Texas Red River Country: The Official Survey of the Headwaters, 1876,* by T. Lindsay Baker, with a foreword by Dan L. Flores; D. Gentry Steele's insightful personal portrait, *Land of the Desert Sun: Texas' Big Bend Country;* and a fascinating natural history study, *The World of the Harvester Ants,* by Stephen Taber. Other 1998 titles included Lee Winniford's *Following Old Fencelines: Tales from Rural Texas,* William E. Reaves, Jr.'s *Texas Art and a Wildcatter's Dream,* Kenneth B. Ragsdale's *Big Bend Country: Land of the Unexpected,* Richard W. Bricker's *Wooden Ships from Texas: A World War I Saga,* and Richard Schroeder's *Texas Signs On: The Early Days of Radio and Television.* This was traditional TAMUP at its best.

Titles reflecting new directions and the increasingly global character of society included *Soviet Defense Spending: A History of CIA Estimates, 1950–1990,* by Noel E. Firth and James H. Noren; Louis Fisher's *The Politics of Shared Power: Congress and the Executive* (fourth edition), Murray Stein's *Transformation: Emer-*

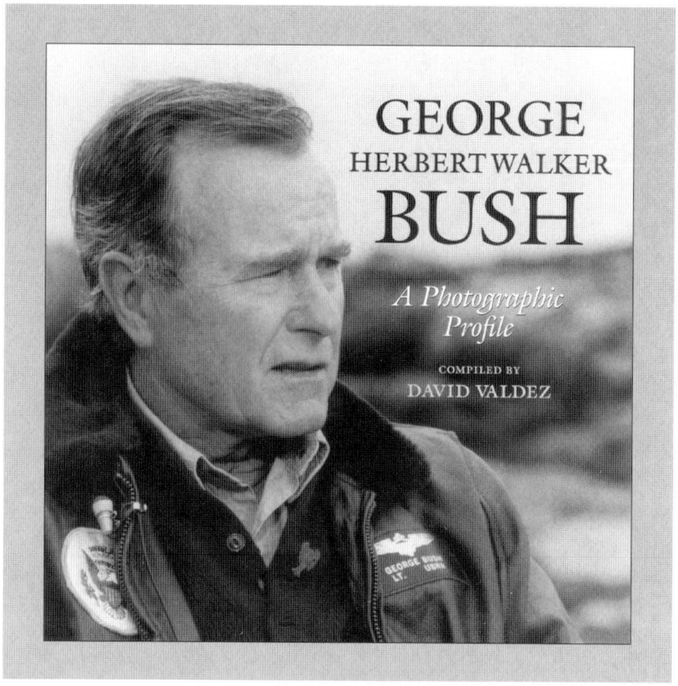

FIG. 35. *The opening of the George Bush Presidential Library on the Texas A&M University campus was a notable event in the fall of 1997. In commemoration of that event, and in cooperation with the Library, the press published* George Herbert Walker Bush: A Photographic Profile *by David Valdez, Bush's personal photographer.*

gence of the Self; and astronomer Ronald A. Schorn's *Planetary Astronomy: From Ancient Times to the Third Millennium.*

In March of 1998, at the Texas State Historical Association meetings in Austin, the Press was able to announce a new series on the history of South Texas, the Canseco-Keck History Series, under the general editorship of Jerry D. Thompson of Texas A&M International University in Laredo. This series was made possible through the generous support of John H. and Ceci Canseco Keck of Laredo, "whose commitment to the study of history," the Press noted in its announcement flier, was "longstanding and notable." The series was intended to focus on South Texas, Borderlands, and Civil War history and included annual publication subsidies for books, as well as research grants to stimulate works in these areas. The first two books in the series, scheduled to appear in spring and fall of 1999, respectively, were *Border Boss: Manuel B. Bravo and Zapato County,* by J. Gilberto Quezada, and a study of Hugh McLeod and the Texan–Santa Fe Expedition (title pending at press time), by Paul Spellman. Two research projects had also been funded for future publication, one on Mexican American landholding in South Texas and the other on the Republic of the Rio Grande.

By the fall of 1998, the list had grown substantially. TAMUP was publishing some forty-five to fifty new titles a year (plus reprints of earlier press titles). The staff, on the other hand, had remained amazingly stable. The first employee ever hired by Frank Wardlaw, Gayla Christiansen, remained, now as marketing manager. Three other staff members (Dianna Hein, Noel Parsons, and Mary Lenn Dixon) had logged more than twenty years each in the organization. The total staff had grown to encompass twenty-two full-time

FIG. 36. *Texas A&M University anthropologist and photographer D. Gentry Steele assembled a fascinating collection of his photographs of the Big Bend for publication in fall 1998. The book,* Land of the Desert Sun: Texas' Big Bend Country, *was number 28 in the Louise Lindsey Merrick Natural Environment Series.*

FIG. 37. *Another illustrated nature book on the spring 1999 list was* Heralds of Spring in Texas, *by Roland H. Wauer, former chief naturalist of Big Bend National Park, active nature writer, and author of the press's books* Naturalist's Big Bend *and* Naturalist's Mexico. *The cover art shown here, a collection of several Texas spring heralds, is by wildlife and nature illustrator Ralph Scott.*

employees, three part-time employees, some dozen student workers, and three student interns.

The growth and success of the press has, of course, depended not only on the vision of its leadership, but also on the competence of its experienced and committed staff. The press has been fortunate in having an unusually low turnover rate and a very talented staff. In addition to those mentioned previously, several other members of the press staff have logged more than five years with the organization.

In the marketing/warehousing department alone, three members have accumulated some thirty-four years among them. Steve Griffis came to the press in 1983 and has served as Texas trade sales and warehouse manager, providing liaison not only with Texas bookstores but with many press authors who have become good friends, and often bringing in leads for new books. Mike Martin joined the press staff in 1986 and is assistant warehouse manager, in which role he has trained and supervised a host of student and part-time workers. For his efforts at the press and as a community volunteer, including coaching basketball teams for Bryan Boys and Girls Clubs, Martin was awarded the President's Meritorious Service award by the university in 1994. Joan Osth first started work at the press as an A&M student in 1993 and was hired full-time in January, 1994, after graduating. Her design skills have been responsible for the press's handsome catalogs since then, among many other assignments she has.

Staff members in other departments have also served well for several years. Johnny Ruiz began work in the finance department in 1984. Wynona Davis and Jackie Thornton joined the order fulfillment staff in 1988 and 1991, respectively. Behind-the-scenes efforts of employees like these have contributed to the smooth functioning of the business end of the press's publishing efforts.

As of October, 1998, full-time or part-time employees were:

Administration: Tom Rotell, director; Linda Salitros, assistant to the director, rights and permissions; Edith Wakefield, receptionist and assistant to editorial.

Acquisitions: Noel Parsons, editor-in-chief; Diana Vance, editorial assistant.

Copyediting: Mary Lenn Dixon, managing editor and acquisitions; Karol Murrah, associate editor; Mia Sanders, assistant editor.

Design: Mary Ann Jacob, design manager.

Production: Susan Pettey, production manager; Kevin Grossman, production and design assistant.

Marketing/Warehouse: Gayla Christiansen, marketing manager; Maureen Creamer, publicity and advertising; Joan Osth, marketing design and exhibits; Steve Griffis, sales and warehouse manager; Gabriel Salas, marketing and sales assistant; Mike Martin, assistant warehouse manager; Stanley Pavlas, warehouse; Yloundas Thompson, warehouse.

Business Operations: Sharon Mills, business operations manager; Wynona Davis, accounts receivable; Lori Ann Bruggman, accounts receivable; Jackie Thornton, order fulfillment.

Finance: Dianna Hein, financial manager; Johnny Ruiz, financial assistant.

In the late fall of 1998, as this book was "going to press," yet another personnel change was announced. Tom Rotell stated his intention to retire in the spring of 1999. Amid accolades praising his accomplishments at the press, the university administration named a committee and began a national search process to choose his successor. By the time this book appears in print, a new chapter will have begun in the press's unfolding history.

Changes occurring at Texas A&M University and in the global society over the past quarter-century have strongly affected TAMUP's affairs, imposing new challenges and requiring changes in the press's operations and programs. That, of course, is the way it should be, because the press is an integral part of the university. From its establishment in 1974, Texas A&M University Press has functioned to implement the university's educational and service mission. During the press's first quarter-century, fundamental changes have been occurring in the field of publishing. Both the elements of university publishing and the general context within which it occurs have changed a great deal. Indeed, as a new era begins in the unknown, challenging, and sometimes threatening world of electronic media, the publishing environment seems more stressful and more competitive.

As it has from the beginning, TAMUP continues to stimulate scholarly productivity of the broadest type on the campus, providing an effective outlet for faculty ideas. It has released important books that have become a significant part of the realm of ideas. The press has conducted a responsible program of regional interpretation, as Wardlaw stressed it must do, and has provided an effective medium for extending the educational thrust of the university. The Texas A&M Press has become an important instrument for enhancing the academic prestige of the university on both the national and international scenes. Its diverse publications have provided moments of pleasure and undoubtedly provoked moments of intense thought and reflection. Already, in its short lifetime, the press has attracted a devoted coterie of patrons, partisans, and readers.

What TAMUP had done has not been easy, and its work is far from complete. Indeed, the press has been a part of the Texas A&M University scene for such a relatively short time that Lloyd Lyman remarked, upon hearing of the project to write its history, that such a history might be premature. For you see, he said, the press has only just begun.

The character of the press is still evolving, as is Texas A&M University as a whole. The university has undergone profound changes in the last twenty-five years. In recent years, the university's enrollment has more than doubled. Today more than forty thousand students, including a substantial number at the graduate level, are enrolled. Participation in the venerable Corps of Cadets now forms part of the student experience for only a small portion of the student body. Wholly coeducational and diversified, Texas A&M has become, in the words of its former president, Frank E. Vandiver, a "world-class" university. The new College of Medicine, which admitted its first class in 1977, soon became a fully accredited, nationally recognized medical school; concomitantly, the Bryan–College Station community became a major regional medical center. The Texas A&M University System, which had only four campuses in 1974, has grown to encompass nine campuses enrolling more than 175,000 students. The nine campuses have a combined annual budget of over one billion dollars. The George Bush Presidential Library, which even before it opened its doors to researchers in 1997 had stimulated new and exciting programs, ideas, and publications, continues to draw unprecedented numbers of visitors.

The world of which Texas A&M University forms part also has changed dramatically. The Cold War ended. NAFTA began operating. Science and medicine made giant advances, while space exploration, satellites, and the electronic media revolutionized communications. The resulting global community and economy have created new visions for humankind.

Having made its beginning and begun its legacy, Texas A&M University Press is poised to explore this challenging new era. As Clarence Day, Jr., cofounder of Yale University Press, said, "Books lie at the heart of scholarship." As he emphasized:

> *The world of books is the most remarkable creation of man. Nothing else that he builds ever lasts. Monuments fall; nations perish; civilizations grow old and die out; and, after an era of darkness, new races build others. But in the world of books are volumes that have seen this happen again and again, and yet live on, still young, still as fresh as the day they were written, still telling men's hearts of the hearts of men centuries dead.*[35]

The university press's assignment will continue to be to publish what is important, maintaining its ability to preserve the significant fruits of intellectual labor, without regard to current commercial value. With this orientation, Texas A&M University Press will continually renew itself. Each new book marks a beginning.

Notes

CHAPTER 1. THE BEGINNING

1. Frank Wardlaw to Jack K. Williams, "The Beginning," Sept. 3, 1974, Texas A&M University Press Files and Records, College Station (hereafter cited as TAMUP).

2. Henry C. Dethloff, *A Centennial History of Texas A&M University, 1876–1976*, 2 vols. (College Station: Texas A&M University Press, 1975), 1:18–19.

3. Frank Wardlaw to Jack Williams, "The Beginning."

4. Frank Wardlaw to W. H. Patterson, Oct. 28, 1975, TAMUP.

5. Ibid.

6. Ibid.

7. Ibid.; Frank Wardlaw to Henry Winkler, Feb. 3, 1975, TAMUP.

8. *Austin American-Statesman*, Mar. 29, 1985; Rosemary Wardlaw, interview by Henry C. Dethloff, Austin, Tex., Apr. 17, 1997.

9. Rosemary Wardlaw, interview.

10. Ibid.; *Battalion*, Jan. 16, 1974.

11. Frank Wardlaw, *"I Have That Honor: Tributes to J. Frank Dobie* (Paisano, Tex., and Biddeford Pool, Me.: Congressional Press, 1965); *Houston Chronicle*, Feb. 19, 1978.

12. Rosemary Wardlaw, interview.

13. Frank Wardlaw, "The Return of Type 22," *Scholarly Publishing* (Apr., 1976): 203–11.

14. Frank Wardlaw to Alfred A. Knopf, Nov. 4, 1974, TAMUP; Elizabeth A. H. John, interview by Henry C. Dethloff, Austin, Tex., Apr. 17, 1997.

15. Rosemary Wardlaw, interview.

16. Lindsey was born in Waxahachie, Texas, in 1922. Within the year, he moved with his family to Houston, where his father went into the insurance business. He grew up in Houston, attended Lamar High School, and, following the advice of friends, enrolled at Texas A&M University in the fall of 1940. He began studying to be an engineer but then decided that he liked economics and accounting better. During his junior year, his entire class was called to military duty. Lindsey was sent to Field Artillery training at Fort Sill, Oklahoma; he finished Officers Candidate School (OCS) and was commissioned. For a time he remained at Fort Sill to train new recruits. In January, 1945, he arrived in Italy, just in time for V-E Day, and his unit speedily was shipped out to the Philippines, where the war

seemed far from over. He was in the Philippines when the atomic bomb was dropped on Hiroshima and Nagasaki, Japan. He then was sent to Japan to serve with the American Army of Occupation. He got back to the states in July, 1946; married Sara Houstoun; and, in January, 1947, enrolled at Texas A&M to finish his degree. John H. Lindsey, interview by Henry C. Dethloff, Houston, Apr. 8, 1997.

17. Frank Wardlaw, "Return of Type 22," 204.

18. Ibid.

19. Lindsey, interview.

20. A 1940 graduate of Emory and Henry College, Jack K. Williams completed a master's degree and a Ph.D. in history there after the war. He began teaching at Clemson University in 1947, rising to the post of vice-president for academic affairs at Clemson before coming to Texas as the state's first commissioner of the Coordinating Board of the Texas College and University System. After a brief stint as vice-president for academic affairs at the University of Tennessee, Williams accepted the post of president of Texas A&M University. Dethloff, *Centennial History,* 2:580–81.

21. Lindsey, interview.

22. Ibid.

23. Ibid.; Frank Wardlaw, "Return of Type 22," 204.

24. Lindsey, interview.

25. Ibid.

26. Ibid.

27. Ibid.

28. Haskell Monroe, conversation with Henry C. Dethloff, Apr. 7, 1997.

29. Lindsey, interview.

30. Frank Wardlaw, "Return of Type 22," 205.

31. Rosemary Wardlaw, interview.

32. Rosemary Wardlaw, interview.

33. Frank Wardlaw to Jack Schulman, Sept. 13, 1974, TAMUP.

34. Frank Wardlaw to Jack Williams, "The Beginning."

35. Ibid.

36. Ibid.; Gayla Christiansen, interview by Henry C. Dethloff, College Station, Apr. 7, 1997.

37. Frank Wardlaw to Jack Williams, "The Beginning."

38. Frank Wardlaw to Richard O.("Buck") Weirus, executive director, Association of Former Students, Sept. 30, 1974, TAMUP.

39. Frank Wardlaw to Jack Williams, "The Beginning"; Frank Wardlaw to Weirus, Sept. 30, 1974; Richard O. ("Buck") Weirus, telephone conversation with Henry C. Dethloff, Apr. 4, 1997; Lindsey, interview.

40. Frank Wardlaw to Tom Cherry, Sept. 18, 1974, TAMUP; Frank Wardlaw to Jack Williams, Oct. 23, 1974, TAMUP.

41. Centennial Committee to Executive Committee, Feb. 10, 1972, in personal files of Henry C. Dethloff.

42. Richard O. ("Buck") Weirus to Dr. J. M. Nance, Oct. 30, 1972, in personal files of Henry C. Dethloff.

43. As the team's reserves dwindled due to injuries during a crucial championship game against Centre College of Kentucky in 1921, Aggie cadet E. King Gill was called from the stands to suit up and be ready to play for A&M. The Aggies went on to win the game, defeating Centre College 22–14 in a great upset victory. Although Gill did not have to play, his willingness to do so became a symbol of Aggies' willingness to serve their school when called upon.

44. Frank Wardlaw to Richard O. ("Buck") Weirus, Sept. 17, 1974, TAMUP; Frank Wardlaw to Jack Williams, Apr. 24, 1975, TAMUP; Frank Wardlaw to Richard O. ("Buck") Weirus, May 1, 1975, TAMUP.

45. Frank Wardlaw to Kenneth Montague, Nov. 20, 1974, TAMUP.

46. Frank Wardlaw to Bob Walker, Feb. 16, 1976, TAMUP; Frank Wardlaw to John G. Pew, Feb. 18, 1976, TAMUP.

47. Frank Wardlaw to J. Harold Dunn, Dec. 12, 1974, TAMUP.

48. Joe H. and Betty Moore, interview by Henry C. Dethloff, Austin, Tex., Apr. 15, 1997.

49. Ibid.

50. Ibid.

51. Ibid.

52. Ibid.

53. Frank Wardlaw to John C. Calhoun, Oct. 4, 1974, TAMUP; Frank Wardlaw to H. D. Hoese, Oct. 4, 1974, TAMUP.

54. Frank Wardlaw to Trustees, Moody Foundation, May 28, 1975, TAMUP.

55. Frank Wardlaw to Edward L. Protz, Moody Foundation, Mar. 15, 1976, TAMUP.

56. Peter's decision to take a job in industry, with Chevron Research in California, led Elizabeth to the Bancroft Library and its rich collections of western and early American documents. The family then moved to Davis, California, where Peter joined the faculty; eventually Elizabeth accepted a part-time teaching position in history at Sacramento State University. That led to a full-time position teaching western history and more intense research on her chosen topic. Eventually the family moved to the University of Texas. Elizabeth did not teach, but the Bexar Archives proved irresistible. Elizabeth A. H. John, interview; Elizabeth A. H. John, "A View from the Spanish Borderlands," *Proceedings of the American Antiquarian Society* 101, pt. 1 (1991): 77–87.

57. John, interview.

58. Ibid.

59. Ibid.

60. Frank Wardlaw to Weirus, May 1, 1975. A less technical grass guide, *Common Texas*

Grasses: An Illustrated Guide, adapted by Gould, was published by Texas A&M University Press three years later, in 1978.

61. Ibid.

62. Ibid.

63. Ibid.

64. Charlotte Phelan, "Making Books in Aggieland," *Houston Post,* Nov. 10, 1974.

65. Frank Wardlaw to Charles E. Cunningham, Sept. 19, 1975, TAMUP.

66. Frank Wardlaw to Louis T. Iglehart, director, University of Tennessee Press, Oct. 29, 1975, TAMUP.

67. Frank Wardlaw to Cunningham.

68. Frank Wardlaw to Donald A. Collins, May 28, 1975, TAMUP.

69. Frank Wardlaw to John C. Calhoun, vice-president for academic affairs, July 2, 1975, TAMUP.

70. Frank Wardlaw to Iglehart.

CHAPTER 2. AIR, EARTH, FIRE, AND WATER

1. Noel R. Parsons, interview by Henry C. Dethloff, College Station, Tex., Apr. 23, 1997.

2. Ibid.

3. Ibid.

4. Ibid.

5. Ibid.

6. Ibid.

7. Frank Wardlaw to Carol Franz, Nov. 17, 1975, TAMUP.

8. Parsons, interview, Apr. 23, 1997; Weirus, telephone conversation.

9. Frank Wardlaw to Jack Williams, "The Beginning."

10. Ibid.

11. Frank Wardlaw to Cunningham.

12. Margaret Ingram to Arthur Orrmont, Oct. 28, 1974, TAMUP.

13. Ibid.; Frank Wardlaw to Dr. R. H. Harrison III, Nov. 21, 1974, TAMUP.

14. Frank Wardlaw to Weirus, May 1, 1975.

15. Frank Wardlaw to Bob Walker, July 11, 1975, TAMUP.

16. Frank Wardlaw to Kenneth Montague, Aug. 29, 1975, TAMUP.

17. Anthony E. Copp, *Regulating Competition in Oil: Government Intervention in the U.S. Refining Industry, 1948–1975,* Texas A&M University Economics Series No. 1 (College Station: Texas A&M University Press, 1976).

18. Frank Wardlaw to Jack Williams, Jan. 6, 1976, TAMUP.

19. Henry C. Dethloff, *Texas A&M University: A Pictorial History, 1876–1996,* 2d ed. (College Station: Texas A&M University Press, 1996), 129.

20. Seventy-fifth Anniversary Committee, *The Agricultural and Mechanical College of Texas, 1876–1951: 75th Anniversary* (College Station: Texas A&M University, 1950), 11.

21. Frank Wardlaw to Bob Walker, Feb. 16, 1976, TAMUP; Frank Wardlaw to Wayne Stark, June 15, 1976, TAMUP.

22. Lloyd G. Lyman to Clyde H. Wells, acting chancellor, Mar. 19, 1979, TAMUP.

23. Frank Wardlaw to Florence Rosengren, Feb. 14, 1977, TAMUP.

24. That same year, Merrick donated $500,000 to Southwest Texas State University to establish an endowed chair in literature. The previous year (1976), this generous lover of nature had given a 4,500-acre ranch near Bandera to the State of Texas' Parks and Wildlife Department for use as a wildlife refuge. *Tyler (Tex.) Morning Telegraph,* Oct. 12, 1977.

25. "Proposed News Release," n.d., enclosed in Frank Wardlaw to John Jefferson, *Texas Parks and Wildlife* Magazine, Apr. 11, 1977, TAMUP.

26. Texas A&M University Press, *Books in Print as of Fall, 1978;* Frank Wardlaw to Jefferson, Apr. 11, 1977; Frank Wardlaw to Louise Lindsey Merrick, June 6, 1977, TAMUP.

27. Frank Wardlaw to William A. Owens, July 29, 1976, TAMUP.

28. Bill Brett, *The Stolen Steers: A Tale of the Big Thicket* (College Station: Texas A&M University Press, 1977).

29. *Junks of Central China: The Spencer Collection of Models at Texas A&M University,* text by J. E. Spencer, foreword by Edwin Doran, Jr., and photographs by Jim Bones, Jr. (College Station: Texas A&M University Press, 1976).

30. Frank Wardlaw to Maud Wilcox, chair, Committee on Membership, Association of American University Presses, Oct. 6, 1976, TAMUP.

31. Frank Wardlaw to Mrs. Richard Underwood, Mar. 15, 1976, TAMUP.

32. Frank Wardlaw to Lloyd Lyman, June 10, 1977, TAMUP.

33. Lloyd Lyman, interview by Henry C. Dethloff, Bandon, Ore., May 29, 1997.

34. Ibid.

35. Ibid.

36. Memo, Papers Relating to the Armed Services Preparedness Investigating Subcommittee, Other People's Statements on Satellites, Senate Papers, Box 356, Lyndon Baines Johnson Presidential Library, Austin, Tex.; *Inquiry into Satellite and Missile Programs: Hearings Before the Preparedness Investigating Subcommittee of the Committee on Armed Services,* 85th Cong., 1st and 2d sess., pt. 1 (Washington, D.C.: U.S. Government Printing Office, 1958), 1–2; Lyndon Baines Johnson, *The Vantage Point: Perspectives on the Presidency, 1963–1969* (New York: Holt, Rinehart and Winston, 1971), 272.

37. Lyman, interview.

38. Ibid.

39. Frank Wardlaw to Jack Williams, July 19, 1978, TAMUP.

40. Ibid.

41. Frank Wardlaw to Jack Williams, Aug. 8, 1978, TAMUP; Jack Williams to Frank Wardlaw, Aug. 8, 1978, TAMUP; Richard ("Buck") Weirus to Jack Williams, Aug. 10, 1978, TAMUP.

42. Jack Williams to Ford D. Albritton, Jr., Oct. 11, 1978, TAMUP.

43. Robert G. Barnes to Frank Wardlaw, May 2, 1978, TAMUP.

44. F. E. Abernethy to Frank Wardlaw, May 17, 1978, TAMUP.

45. Jim Bones to Frank Wardlaw, May 31, 1978, TAMUP.

46. Gayla Christiansen to Frank Wardlaw, June 26, 1978, TAMUP.

47. John Henry Faulk to Frank Wardlaw, May 9, 1978, TAMUP; Llerena Friend to Frank Wardlaw, May, 1978, TAMUP; George Fuermann to Frank Wardlaw, May 30, 1978, TAMUP; Leon Hale to Frank Wardlaw, May, 1978, TAMUP.

48. Frank E. Vandiver to Frank Wardlaw, May 23, 1978, TAMUP.

49. Noel and Kris Parsons to Frank Wardlaw, n.d., TAMUP.

50. Lyman to Frank Wardlaw, June 1, 1978, TAMUP.

51. Lyman to Jack Williams, Oct. 5, 1978, TAMUP.

52. News release written by Lane B. Stephenson, University Relations, Texas A&M University, College Station, Nov. 29, 1978, TAMUP.

53. Frank Wardlaw to Betty and Joe Moore, Nov. 10, 1979, Personal Papers of Betty and Joe Moore, Austin, Tex.

54. Parsons, interview, Apr. 23, 1997.

55. Ibid.

56. Lyman, telephone interview by Henry C. Dethloff, May 5, 1997; "Chancellor Williams Resigns," *Texas Aggie,* Feb., 1979, 20.

57. Lyman to John W. Caple, Mar. 1, 1979, TAMUP; Jerry Cooper, telephone interview by Henry C. Dethloff, May 19, 1997; News release, Office of Public Information, Texas A&M University, College Station, Mar. 2, 1979.

58. News release, Office of Public Information, Texas A&M University, College Station, Mar. 2, 1979.

CHAPTER 3. UP FROM THE ASHES

1. Lyman to Caple, Mar. 1, 1979.

2. "Chancellor Williams Resigns," *Texas Aggie,* Feb., 1979, 20.

3. Lyman to Wells, Mar. 19, 1979.

4. Don Collins, telephone interview by Henry C. Dethloff, June 20, 1997.

5. Ibid.

6. Ibid.

7. "Regents Argue about Damaged Home," *Bryan–College Station (Tex.) Eagle,* Mar. 27, 1979.

8. Lyman to Ford D. Albritton, Jr., June 20, 1979, TAMUP.

9. John H. Lindsey to Texas A&M University Press Advisory Committee, July 12, 1979, TAMUP.

10. Frank Vandiver to John H. Lindsey, Aug. 24, 1979, TAMUP. Lyman to Univer-

sity Press Advisory Council, Aug. 9, 1979, TAMUP; Clyde H. Wells to John H. Lindsey, Aug. 20, 1979, TAMUP.

11. Texas A&M University System, "Request for Construction Project," Oct. 8, 1980, TAMUP.

12. Lyman to B. D. Dick, Nov. 28, 1979, TAMUP.

13. Donald A. Collins to Lyman, May 26, 1980, TAMUP.

14. Ibid.

15. Ibid.

16. Ibid.

17. Ibid.

18. Ibid.

19. Ibid.

20. Collins, telephone interview; Press Distribution Agreements, TAMUP.

21. Frank Wardlaw to the Faculty Advisory Committee, Sept. 29, 1976, TAMUP; Noel Parsons, interview by Henry C. Dethloff, College Station, Tex., June 20, 1997.

22. Mary Lenn Dixon, interview by Henry C. Dethloff, College Station, Tex., June 5, 1997.

23. Ibid.

24. Ibid.

25. Ibid.

26. Ibid.

27. Ibid.

28. Margaret Ingram, memo to Lyman: "Proposed Changes in Editorial Department," n.d., TAMUP.

29. Dixon, interview; June 5, 1997.

30. "Candidates for Spring 1981 List," Feb. 7, 1980, TAMUP.

31. Ibid.; "Candidates for the Fall 1981 List," Feb. 7, 1980, TAMUP.

32. "Mss. Under Consideration, In-House," Aug. 23, 1979; "Revisions in the Works, Not In-house," Oct. 23, 1979; "Likely Titles for Future Lists," Apr. 24, 1979; all TAMUP.

33. Lyman, interview.

34. Texas A&M University System, "Request for Construction Project," Oct. 8, 1980; "Program of Requirements for a Texas A&M University Press Building, the Texas A&M University System, Project No. 1-2367," Jan. 1, 1981, TAMUP.

35. William N. Stokes, Jr., quoted in "Program of Requirements," 1.

36. Student Senate Bill 81-026-(5) cited in *Battalion,* Nov. 6, 1981; "Warped," cartoon by Scott McCullar, *Battalion,* Nov. 6, 1981.

37. Dixon, interview, June 5, 1997.

38. Lyman to F. W. R. Hubert, Mar. 10, 1981, TAMUP.

39. "Briefing on the Texas A&M University Press for TAMUS [Texas A&M University System] Board of Regents," June 10, 1982, TAMUP.

40. Ibid.; Lyman, interview.

41. *Remembering Bill: A Tribute to William H. Shearer (1950–1996), Texas Publisher* (Fredericksburg, Tex.: Shearer Publishing, 1997), 1–116.

42. Ibid.

43. Ibid.; Karl Kilian, Houston, Oct. 30, 1996, TAMUP.

44. Lyman, interview. See Building Files, TAMUP.

45. John Lindsey to Lyman, May 26, 1983, TAMUP; Frank E. Vandiver to Lyman, May 31, 1983, TAMUP.

46. Sterling C. Evans to Lyman, n.d., TAMUP.

47. John H. Lindsey Building Dedication files, Sept. 17, 1983, TAMUP.

48. "A&M Press," *Austin American-Statesman,* Sept. 25, 1983.

49. *Dallas Morning News,* Aug. 28, 1983. Collins, telephone interview.

50. Frank H. Wardlaw Collection of Texas Art (descriptive files), TAMUP.

51. Memorandum to the Advisory Council, Texas A&M University Press, signed by Chester Kerr, August Frugé, Jack Schulman, and Jack Goellner, Sept. 14, 1983, TAMUP.

52. Dixon, interview, June 5, 1997.

CHAPTER 4. MAKING BOOKS

1. Jimmy Carlysle (Jim) Billingsley, interview by Henry C. Dethloff, College Station, May 10, 1997.

2. Ibid.

3. Ibid.

4. Ibid.

5. Ibid.

6. Quotations from J. Frank Dobie to Tom Lea, in foreword to *The Art of Tom Lea,* comp. Kathleen G. Hjerter (College Station: Texas A&M University Press, 1989), ix–xi.

7. Billingsley, interview; *Art of Tom Lea,* i. Robert Justus Kleberg, Jr., was an owner and director of the legendary King Ranch from 1935 until his death in 1974. Texas A&M University awarded Kleberg an honorary degree in agriculture in 1941 for his contributions to Texas' cattle and livestock industry. Much later, the university named the Kleberg Animal and Food Science Center for him.

8. Billingsley, interview.

9. Halford Mackinder's views on geography influenced world politics and military affairs for much of the first half of the twentieth century. Information on Baker and Harrison from Noel Parsons, Working Manuscript Review Files, TAMUP.

10. *Texas A&M University Press Catalog,* Fall, 1985, p. 4.

11. Ibid.; *Texas A&M University Press Catalog,* Spring, 1986.

12. *Texas A&M University Press Catalog,* Fall, 1985.

13. *Texas A&M University Press Catalog,* Spring, 1986; *Texas A&M University Press Catalog,* Fall, 1986.

14. *Texas A&M University Press Catalog,* Fall, 1986, 6.

15. Mary Ann Jacob, interview by Henry C. Dethloff, College Station, Tex., July 9, 1997.

16. Susan Pettey-Pearce, interview by Henry C. Dethloff, College Station, Tex., July 9, 1997.

17. Dianna Hein, interview by Henry C. Dethloff, College Station, Tex., July 7, 1997.

18. Ibid.

19. Ibid.

20. See "Gathering of the Herd" invitations, notes, and records for 1985, TAMUP.

21. Sharon Yvonne Pavlas, interview by Henry C. Dethloff, College Station, Tex., July 7, 1997. Pavlas married Craig Mills in 1998.

22. Clayton W. Williams, *Texas' Last Frontier: Fort Stockton and the Trans-Pecos, 1861–1895*, ed. Ernest Wallace (College Station: Texas A&M University Press, 1982).

23. Elizabeth Silverthorne, *Plantation Life in Texas* (College Station, Texas: Texas A&M University Press, 1986), dust jacket.

24. Joe H. and Betty Moore, interview; Lyman, interview. See James A. Michener, *Texas* (New York: Random House, 1985), vii–xiii.

25. Lloyd Lyman, "A Proposal for a Texas Social History Series," Oct., 1983, TAMUP; Lloyd Lyman, "Notes from a Conversation with John Kings," Nov. 11, 1983, TAMUP.

26. Clayton W. Williams, Jr., to Lyman, Nov. 15, 1983, TAMUP.

27. *Texas A&M University Press, Fall 1987.*

28. *Texas A&M University Press, Spring 1987.*

29. Lyman, interview.

30. Texas A&M University Press, *Complete List of Books in Print, December 31, 1987*, 7, 9.

31. *Texas A&M University Press, Spring 1988.*

32. Ibid.

33. Mary Carolyn Hollers George, *O'Neil Ford, Architect* (College Station: Texas A&M University Press, 1992), acknowledgments and dust jacket.

34. *San Antonio Express-News,* Oct. 2, 1988, p. 6-H. Lyman, interview.

35. Lyman, interview.

36. Frank E. Vandiver, remarks on Lloyd Lyman's retirement, Aug. 28, 1988, TAMUP.

37. John Frederick Stetter, interview by Henry C. Dethloff, College Station, Tex., June 15, 1997.

38. Ibid.

39. Ibid.

40. Ibid.

41. Ibid.

42. Briefing Book on Texas A&M University Press, prepared for President William H. Mobley, Sept., 1988, TAMUP.

43. Ibid.

44. Ibid.

45. Ibid.

46. Ibid.

47. *Texas A&M University Press, Spring 1989.*

48. Ibid.

49. Ibid.

50. Diana Lee Vance, interview by Henry C. Dethloff, College Station, Tex., July 16, 1997.

51. Hein, interview.

52. *Texas A&M University Press, Spring 1989; Texas A&M University Press, Spring 1990.*

53. Patsy McDonald Spaw, ed., *The Texas Senate,* vol. 1: *Republic to Civil War, 1836–1861* (College Station: Texas A&M University Press, 1990), xi–xiii; William P. Hobby, foreword to *The Texas Senate,* vol. 1: *Republic to Civil War, 1836–1861,* ed. Patsy McDonald Spaw (College Station: Texas A&M University Press, 1990), ix–x; Stetter, interview.

54. *Texas A&M University Press, Fall 1997,* 7; Texas A&M University Press, *Complete List of Books in Print, 1997,* 52.

55. *Texas A&M University Press, Fall 1991,* 3–15.

56. Ibid.

57. Stetter, interview.

58. Mary Elaine Miller, interview by Henry C. Dethloff, College Station, Tex., July 17, 1997.

59. Ibid.

60. Ibid.

61. Ibid.

62. Ibid.

63. Karol Murrah, interview by Henry C. Dethloff, College Station, Tex., July 16, 1997.

64. Miller, interview.

65. Ibid.

CHAPTER 5. STRATEGIC PLANNING

1. Thomas M. Rotell, interview by Henry C. Dethloff, College Station, Tex., July 16, 1997.

2. Ibid.

3. Ibid.

4. Ibid.

5. Ibid.

6. Ibid.

7. Ibid.

8. Ibid.

9. Ibid.

10. Mary Lenn Dixon, interview by Henry C. Dethloff, College Station, Tex., July 29, 1997.

11. *Bryan–College Station (Tex.) Eagle,* Dec. 14, 1995.

12. Dixon, interview, July 29, 1997; Notes, "Hughes Series, Proposals and Manuscripts," TAMUP.

13. *Texas A&M University Press, Fall/Winter 1997,* 16–17; also see Texas A&M University Press, *Books in Print, 1997.*

14. Karol Murrah, interview by Henry C. Dethloff, College Station, July 29, 1997.

15. *Texas A&M University Press, Fall/Winter 1995,* 3; *Texas A&M University Press, Fall/Winter 1996,* 9.

16. *Texas A&M University Press, Fall/Winter 1995,* 5.

17. Ibid., 6–11.

18. *Texas A&M University Press, Fall/Winter 1996,* 1–11.

19. *Texas A&M University Press News* 2 (Spring, 1997): 2.

20. Ibid.

21. Ibid.; *Texas A&M University Press, Fall/Winter 1997,* 14.

22. Rotell, interview.

23. Maureen Creamer, interview by Henry C. Dethloff, College Station, Tex., July 29, 1997.

24. Ibid.

25. Rotell, interview

26. Ibid.

27. Ibid.

28. Ibid.

29. Ibid.

30. Memorandum, Thomas M. Rotell to Dr. Ronald G. Douglas, via Dr. William L. Perry, Apr. 15, 1997, TAMUP.

31. Ibid.

32. Ibid.

33. *Texas A&M University Press, Spring/Summer 1997,* 3.

34. *Texas A&M University Press, Fall/Winter 1997,* 3.

35. Clarence Day, cited in D. Kimball Smith, "Publishing: The Books That Must Be Done," *Yale Alumni Magazine,* Apr., 1984, 24.

Index

A&M Mothers' Club, 116
Abernethy, Francis E., 54
Abilene, Tex., 104
Adams, John A., Jr., 61
Adkisson, Perry Lee, 111
Albanese, Robert A., 96
Albritton, Ford D., Jr., 10, 53, 64
Amarillo, Tex., 22
American Association for State and Local History, 107
American Institute of Graphic Arts, 17
American Institute of Nautical Archeology. *See* Institute of Nautical Archeology
American Multi-Cinema, Inc., 15
American Ornithologists' Union, 113
American Society of Mechanical Engineers, 107
Appleman, Roy E., 103
architecture, 106–107, 130
Association of American University Presses, 7, 30, 33, 36, 46, 48, 51, 107
Association of Former Students. *See* Texas A&M University
Association of Former Students Centennial Series, 25
Atlanta, Ga., 116
Austin, Tex., 93, 98, 101
Autry, Gene, 93
awards, 107, 110

Bailey, Florence Merriam, 112
Baker, T. Lindsay, 96–97, 133
Baldwin, Fred, 105
Bandon, Oreg., 107
Barham, Dohn, 69
Barker History Center, 102
Barnes, Robert, 54
Bartsch, William H., 126
Bass, George F., 75–76
Battalion, The, 78
Baxter, David, 43
Baylor University Press, 131
Beaugez, Don, 70, 99
Beavers, Randell A., 115
Bedicek, Roy, 7
Bexar Collection, 26
Big Bend National Park, 136
Biggers, John Thomas, 86
Billingsley, Jimmy Carlyle (Jim), 93–95, 98, 101–102, 112
Blackstock, Graham, 26
Blackwelder, Julia K., 106
Blouet, Brian W., 96
Bones, Jim, 21, 36, 46, 54
bonfire, 78–79
Booth, Herb, 117
Borderlands studies, 130
Bowen, Ray M., 118
Boyce, Robert S., 78
Boynton, Rosemary Leonard, 7
Boy Scouts of America, 97
Bradley, General Omar, 41
Brands, H. W. (Bill), 124
Brannen, J. P., 127
Brazos River, 47
Brett, Bill, 43–45
Bricker, Richard W., 133
Bright, H. R. (Bum), 84
British Museum, 128
Brown, Marbury Hill, 87
Bruggman, Lori Ann, 137

Bryan Boys and Girls Clubs, 137
Bryant, Keith L., Jr., 75
Bryant, Vaughn, 96
Buchanan, James M., 41
Buenger, Walter L., 98
Burch, Robert W., 115
Bush, George Herbert Walker, 134. *See also* George Bush Presidential Library
Bush Presidential Library. *See* George Bush Presidential Library
Bywaters, Jerry, 86

C. A. Brannen Series, 127
Caddy, Douglas, 104
Calhoun, John C., 33, 45
California Fruit Growers Exchange, 49
California Institute of Technology, 49
California State University at Sacremento, 108
Cambodia, 42
Cambridge University, 15
Cambridge University Press, 15, 88
Canseco-Keck History Series, 134
Caperton, Sen. Kent A., 84
Caple, John, 53
Carey, Robin, 112
Carpenter, Liz, 115
Carr, Karen, 126
Carter, George, 37
Cartwright, Thomas C., 96
Cash, Harvey, 53
Cat's Pajamas, 99
Centennial Series, 20, 39, 114, 119. *See also* Texas A&M University: Association of Former Students
Center for the Advancement of Studies in Architecture, 114
Charles and Elizabeth Prothro Texas Photography Series, 104–105, 113
Cherry, Tom D., 18
Cherry, Bob, 20
China, 49
Chinese junks (boats), 45
Christiansen, Gayla Eppright, 15, 36, 54, 64, 70, 77, 81, 98, 112, 130–31, 135, 137
Cigar, Norman, 125
Civilian Conservation Corps (CCC), 6
Civil War, 42
Clark, Ted L., 43
Clayton Wheat Williams Texas Life Series, 101, 114
Clayton W. Williams, Jr. Alumni Center, 107
Clifford, Craig Edward, 97
Clinton, William Jefferson (Bill), 124
Cohen, Philip J., 125
Cold War, 51–52, 125, 128, 139
Coleman, John S., Jr., 55
Collins, Donald A., 32, 36, 64, 66–71, 98, 100
Collins, Fenis F., 86
Columbia (S.C.) *Record,* 6
Columbia University, 122
Columbia University Press, 54
Conkwright, B. J., 94
Cook, Scott, 132
Cooper, Jerry, 39, 64
Copp, E. Anthony, 40
Costa, Richard Hauer, 113
Cowboy Hall of Fame, 107
Cox, Elenor, 37, 96
Cox, Mike, 110
Creamer, Maureen, 128–29, 137
Crisp, James E., 30
Crockett, Davy, 30
Cunningham, Charles E., 38

Dallas, Tex., 126
Darnell, Rezneat, 24, 37
Dartmouth Medical School, 113
Daughters of the Republic of Texas, 110
Davis, Edwin Adams, 126
Davis, Wynona, 137
Dawson, Joseph G., III, 126
Day, Clarence, Jr., 139
Debakey, Michael, 39
DeFrank, Thomas M., 123
Dethloff, Henry C., 96, 115
Dexter, Mich., 93
Dixon, Mary Lenn, 73–74, 111–12, 124, 135, 137
Dobie, Bertha, 10
Dobie, J. Frank, 7, 10, 95, 97
Doran, Edwin, Jr., 45, 77
Downs, Jo Alice, 26

Dozier, Otis, 87
Driscoll, Mrs. Chan, 53
Duncan Field, 78–79
Dunn, J. Harold, 53
DX Sunray Oil Company, 94
Dyal, Donald, 96, 115

Early, Charity Adams, 113
Eastern European Studies, 125, 130
Edwards, Chet, 85, 114
Edwards, George C., III, 124
Eisenhower, Dwight David, 51
electronic media, 72–73, 120
Elementary and Secondary Education Act, 51
Elma Dill Russell Spencer Series on the West and Southwest, 42
Evans, Sterling C., 53, 66, 78, 84
Exley, Jo Ella Powell, 106

Faculty Advisory Committee. *See* Texas A&M University Press
Faulk, John Henry, 54
Fearing, Kelly, 87
Firth, Noel E., 133
Fisch, Louise Ann, 126
Fisher, Louis, 124, 133
Flagstaff, Ariz., 108
Flores, Dan L., 133
Ford, O'Neil, 106–107
Ford Foundation, 52
Fort Worth, Tex., 69
Frank H. Wardlaw Collection of Texas Art, 85–88
Franks, Kenny A., 97
Frantz, Joe B., 110
Frary, Michael, 44, 86
Fredericksburg, Tex., 81
Freeman, Clyde, 20
Friend, Llerena, 26, 54
Fripp Island, 57, 85
Fruge, August, 48–49
Fuermann, George, 55
Fulgham, Geneve, 114
Fullerton Company, 24
Furubotn, Eirik G., 37
Gachechiladze, Revaz, 125
Gage, E. Dean, 116, 118
Gathering of the Herd, 100
Gathright Hall, 86
G.I. Bill, 52
Gibson, Jerry, 96
General Dynamics, 69
Gentry, Diane Koos, 106
George, Mary Carolyn Hollers, 106–107
George Bush Presidential Library, 123–24, 132, 134, 139
George Bush School of Government and Public Service, 123; Center for Leadership Studies, 123; Center for Presidential Studies, 123
George Mason University, 124
Georgetown University Press, 51
Gervasi, Frank, 87
Gibson, Fred, 11
Goellner, Jack, 88
Goldman, Peter, 123
Gould, Frank W., 28–29
Gould, Lucile Bridges, 29
Graves, John, 28, 36
Gregory, Keith, 70
Grider, Sylvia, 96
Griffis, Steve, 136, 137
Grimaila, Raymond M., 16–17, 36, 69, 93
Great Depression, 6, 22, 23, 121
Grey, Zane, 97
Grossman, Kevin, 137
Guerin, John William, 87
Guilmartin, John G., Jr., 126

Hale, Leon, 55–56, 81, 130–31
Hall, Kenneth R., 96
Hall, Linda, 77
Hamilton, Tex., 73, 104
Hansen, Arthur, 82, 84
Harbison, Helen Sewell, 106
Harbison, Pell, 106
Hargrove, Sharon, 113
Harrison, Billy R., 96
Harry Ranson Humanities Research Center, 48
Hart Graphics, 93
Harvard University Press, 53

Heath, Fred, 118, 122
Heaton, Homer Lloyd, 19
Hein, Dianna, 99–101, 112, 135
Heldenfels, H. C., 53
Helen C. Kleberg Foundation, 95
Higgins, Patillo, 113
Hill, John R., Jr., 53, 115
Hill, Peggy Sloan, 115
Hiller, Ilo, 114
Hirshfield House, 64, 88–89
History Book Club, 41
Hobbs, N.M., 24
Hobby, Bill, 114
Hoese, H. D., 24–25
Hoey, William, 87
Hofsommer, Don L., 97
Holland, Ada Morehead, 106
Hollon, W. Eugene, 47
Horsley, Graham, 37
Hotard Hall, 79
Houston, Tex., 98, 128, 131
Hubert, Frank, 20, 66–67, 77–81, 124
Huebner, Klaus H., 103
Hughes, Holly Oldfield, 124
Hughes, Joseph V., Jr., 124
Hull, Tex., 43
Hutson-Tillotson College, 8

Iglehart, Louis, 94
Ingram, Margaret, 15, 36, 74
Institute of Nautical Archeology, 75–76
insurance, 104
Irons, William, 128
Isle of Cypress, 75

Jackson, Stonewall, 132
Jacob, Mary Ann Flusche, 98, 137
Jacobs, Louis, 126
Jefferson, John, 43
Joe and Betty Moore Texas Art Series, 25, 47, 56, 88, 117
John, Elizabeth Ann (Harper), 25–27, 36
John and Sara Lindsey Series in the Arts and Humanities, 106
John E. Conner Museum, 70
John H. Lindsey Texas A&M University Press Building, 84–88
Johns Hopkins University Press, 88
Johnson, Lady Bird, 92, 100
Johnson, Lyndon B., 51, 133
Junction City, Kans., 7
junks, 45
Justin Industries, 108

Kapadia, Valoo, 29
Kansas City, Mo., 15
Keck, Ceci Canseco, 134
Keck, John H., 34
Kenneth E. Montague Series in Oil and Business History, 40, 47–48, 97
Kent State University Press, 51
Kerr, Chester, 88
Kilham, Lawrence, 112
King, Betty, 114
King Ranch, 95
Kleberg, Robert J., Jr., 95
Knopf, Alfred A., 8
Kofalk, Harriet, 112
Korea, 42, 94, 103
Kotak, Conrad, 128
Krueger, Carl C., Jr., 53

Lamar High School, 9
Lambert, Paul F., 97
La Vere, David, 132
Laxalt, Paul, 108
Laxalt, Robert, 108
Lea, Tom, 15, 17, 94–95, 97
Lester, William, 87
Lewie, William H., 10
Lindow man, 128
Lindsey, John H., 8–13, 17, 21, 35, 53, 56, 64–66, 84–86, 100, 106–107, 132
Lindsey, Sara, 11–13, 21, 106–107, 132
Linotype, 72
Long, Meredith, 117
Long, Russell C., 96
Lottinville, Savoie, 94
Louise Lindsey Merrick Natural Environment Series, 42–43, 113, 114, 126, 135

Louisiana State University Press, 47–48
Loving, Jerome M., 37
Loyola University (New Orleans), 116
Lubbock Oil Mill, 78
Lyman, Lea, 48–50, 107
Lyman, Lloyd, 48–50, 52–102, 104, 106–109, 122, 138

McAshan, Mrs. Maurice, 53
McCandless, Barbara, 105
McCullar, Michael, 106
McDaniel, Robert W., 113
McDougal, Ivan Ellis, 87
McEachran, John, 24–25
McGill University Press, 51
McGucken, William, 115
McGuire, Jack, 81
McIntosh, Michael, 117
McMurtry, Larry, 97
McWhiney Foundation Press, 131
Macmillan Publishing Company, 122
Marks, Paula Mitchell, 113
Martin, Mike, 137
Massachusetts Institute of Technology Press, 51
Matthews, Tom, 123
Maurice, S. Charles, 96
Mauro, Garry, 110
Maverick, Mary, 113
Maverick, Sam, 113
Max C. Fleischmann Series in Great Basin Natural History, 108
Medford, Oreg., 49, 108
Medhurst, Martin J., 124
Merrick, Louise Lindsey, 42
Meštrović, Stjepan G., 125
Metzner, Edward P., 126
Michener, James A., 101–102, 121
Michigan State University, 116
Midas, 128
Midland, Tex., 22
military history, 102–103, 106, 126, 130, 134. *See also* Military History Series; *related wars*
Military History Series, 102–103, 126
Miller, Edward G., 126
Miller, Jarvis E., 52, 54, 65
Miller, Mark, 123
Miller, Mary, 116–23
Mills, Sharon Yvonne (Pavlas), 100–101, 137
Mobley, William H., 109–10, 114, 116
Monroe, Haskell, 13, 28, 32, 37, 64, 95
Montague, Kenneth E., 21–22, 35, 40, 53, 56
Montague Petroleum History Series, 25, 77
Moody, W. L., Jr., 25. *See also* W. L. Moody, Jr., Natural History Series
Moody College of Marine Sciences and Maritime Resources, 45
Moody Foundation, 25, 104
Moore, Betty Jane (Monthaven), 22–25, 54, 56, 64, 89, 92–93, 100–102
Moore, Gen. George, 56
Moore, Joe Hiram, 22–25, 35, 53–54, 56, 64, 84, 88–89, 92–93, 100–102
Moore, Richard, 24
Moorehead, Max, 26
Mosher, Edward J., 53
Mott, Lawrence V., 127
Mount Holyoke College, 15
Murr, Andrew, 123
Murrah, Karol, 118, 125, 137
Museum of Northern Arizona, 108
Myers, Sandra L., 106

Nance, Joseph Milton, 19–20
Nash, Sunny, 126
National Aeronautics and Space Administration Act of 1958, 51
National Defense Education Act, 51
National Endowment for the Humanities, 51
National Merit Scholars, 12
National Science Foundation, 51
natural history, 112, 114, 125–27, 130, 136. *See also* Clayton Wheat Williams Texas Life Series; Louise Lindsey Merrick Natural Environment Series
natural science, 130
Nautical Archeology Series, 75, 130. *See also* Studies in Nautical Archeology
Neave, Richard, 128
Nevada City, Oreg., 108
New Deal, 5

New Mexico, 26, 106
New Orleans, La., 116
New York, 18
Nixon, Richard M., 51
Noggle, Anne, 104, 113
Nolan, Keith William, 126
Noren, James H., 133
Northwestern University, 128
Nunn, Ancel, 87

Obregon, Alvaro, 75
O'Connel, James F., 128
Oertling, Thomas J., 127
Ohio State University, 121
Ohio University Press, 51
Oklahoma College for Women, 26
Oklahoma oil, 77
Organization of Petroleum Exporting Countries (OPEC), 4, 40
Orlando, Fla., 132
Osth, Joan, 137
Owens, William A., 43

Parsons, Noel, 33, 35–36, 55, 64, 104, 111–12, 135, 137
Patterson, 4
Pavlas, Stanley, 137
Peace Corps, 7
Peacock, Howard, 113
Pearl Harbor, 47
Peel, Gen. Wesley E., 78
Pena, Jose Erique de la, 30
Pennington, Campbell W., 96
Pennsylvania State University, 121
Pennsylvania State University Press, 51
Perry, Carmen, 30
Pershing, General John J., 41–42, 132
petroleum, 21–22, 97, 102, 113
Pettey, Susan, 98, 112, 137
Pfiffner, James P., 124
Phenix, Harold, 87
Philip of Macedon, 128
Phillabaum, Les, 47
Phillips, Clinton A., 95–96
Pilkington, William T. (Tom), 97
Pingenot, Ben E., 113
Pittman, Blair, 43
Poland, 125
Polokhalo, Volodymyr, 125
Portland, Oreg., 49
Powell, Donald B. 119
Powell, Mary Jo, 119
Prag, John, 128
Prairie View A&M University, 54
Pratt, Joseph, 96, 98
Presidential Rhetoric Series, 124
pressmark, 15, 17
Price, Alvin A., 37, 96
Princeton University, 116
Prothro, Elizabeth, 104
Pryor, Cactus, 81
Purdue University, 82

Quantrill, Malcolm, 114–15
Quezada, J. Gilberto, 135
Quinn, Frederick, 125

Ragsdale, Kenneth B., 133
Random House, 122
Rascoe, Stephen T., 87
Ray, Sammy, 96
Reaves, William E., Jr., 133
Reed College, 49
Republic of Texas, 20
Rhoades, Weldon E., 42
Rhyne, V. Thomas, 37
Rice Hotel, 9
Rice University, 28, 66, 128
Rice University Press, 70, 104
Richardson, Herbert H., 111, 116
Richter, William L., 103
Riesman, David, 41
Robinson, Willard B., 106–107
Rodenberger, Lou, 81
Rogers, Mondel, 22, 87
Romieniec, Edward John, 19
Roosevelt, Theodore, 124
Rosen, David, 111
Rosengren, Florence, 42, 53
Rotell, Thomas M., 121–24, 127–29, 137–38

Rowley, William D., 97
Rudder, James Earl, 10, 19
Ruiz, Johnny, 137
Rundell, Walter, Jr., 21–22, 47–48
Rutgers University Press, 5

Saatcamp, Herman J., 115
Saint Louis, Mo., 128
Salas, Gabriel, 137
Salitros, Linda, 130, 137
Salomen Brothers, 40
Samson, Charles H., 78, 81
San Antonio College, 107
San Antonio Conservation Society, 107
Sanders, Mia, 137
Schiwetz, E. M. "Buck," 10, 13, 27–28, 35, 61, 85–86
Schmidley, David J., 43, 96, 113–14
Scholarly Publishing, 8
Schorn, Ronald A., 134
Schroeder, Richard, 133
Schulman, Jack, 15, 88
Scranton, Pa., 121
Sepulpa, Okla., 93
Series in the Presidency and Leadership Studies, 124
Seton, Ernest Thomas, 97
Shafer, Harry J., 128
Shaw, Charles, 101
Shearer, Bill, 64, 69, 77, 81–82
Shearer Publishing Company, 81
Shell Oil Company, 23
Silverthorne, Elizabeth A., 101, 114
Simmons, Joe J., III, 127
Shoal Creek Publishers, 81
Short, C. Brant, 113
Shuffler, Henderson, 20
Shuler Museum of Palentology, 126
Siringo, Charles A., 113
Skutch, Alexander F., 126
Smith, Emily Guthrie, 87
Smith, F. Todd, 127
Smith, Joyce, 113
Smith, Norman, 6
Smith, Robert, 116
Snyder, William P., 96
Sons of the Republic of Texas, 110
Southern Historical Association, 28
Southern Illinois University Press, 51
Southern Methodist University, 86, 126
Southern Methodist University Press, 70, 104
South Pacific, 101
South Texas. *See* Canseco-Keck History Series
Southwest Landmarks, 97
Soviet Union, 51, 125
Sowls, Lyle K., 127
Spanish-American War, 41
Spaw, Patsy, 114
Spellman, Paul, 135
Spencer, Elma Dill Russell, 42
Spencer, Joseph E., 45–46
Spencer Collection of Model Chinese Junks, 45–46
Spindletop Exploration Company, 124
Spruce, Everett Franklin, 87
Sputnik I, 51
Stark, Wayne, 41
Steele, D. Gentry, 128, 133, 135
Stein, Murray, 133
Stephenville, Tex., 69
Stetter, John Frederick ("Rick"), 108–12, 114–16
Stillwell, Hallie Crawford, 115
Stokes, William N., Jr., 56, 78
Stranges, Anthony N., 77
Strawser, Robert P., 37
Studies in Architecture and Culture, 114
Studies in Nautical Archeology, 127
Swanson, Eric R., 126
Sweetwater, Tex., 22

Taber, Stephen, 133
Tarleton State University, 54, 69, 96–97
Tarleton State University Southwestern Studies in the Humanities, 96–97
Teachers College Press, 122
Teer, James G., 24, 37, 42
Teglas, Csaba, 125
Temple University Press, 51
Texas A&I University (Texas A&M University-Kingsville), 70

Texas Almanac, 131
Texas A&M Anthropology Series, 127–28
Texas A&M International University at Laredo, 134
Texas A&M University: Agricultural Experiment Station, 28, 52; Agricultural Extension Service, 70; Association of Former Students, 9, 17, 20, 22, 25, 30, 39, 53, 61, 93; Board of Directors, 12–13, 19; Board of Directors Building, 13, 14, 58–61, 64–66, 85; Board of Regents, 53–54, 59, 61, 64, 77, 80–82, 84, 118; College of Business Administration, 96; College of Education, 66; College of Medicine, 139; College of Veterinary Medicine, 102; Computing Services, 70; Corps of Cadets, 139; Development Foundation, 21, 39–40; Economics Series, 40; Engineering Extension Service, 15; Forest Service, 70; Galveston, 96; Hirshfield-Moore House, 88; Hotard Hall, 79; John H. Lindsey Texas A&M University Press Building, 84–87; Libraries, 118; Military History Series, 42; Moody College of Marine Sciences and Maritime Resources, 45; Nautical Archeology Series, 75; Office of Continuing Education, 15; Office of Facilities Planning and Construction, 82; Office of University Development, 102; Permanent University Fund, 78; Printing Center, 98; Reed McDonald Building, 64; Riverside Annex, 66; Sea Grant College, 45; University Available Fund, 78, 80
Texas A&M University at Commerce, 127
Texas A&M University at Kingsville, 127
Texas A&M University at Texarkana, 127
Texas A&M University Press: Advisory Council, 53–54, 56, 61, 63, 64, 66, 77, 81, 110, 127; distribution agreement, 70–71; Consortium, 130; Executive Committee, 112; Faculty Advisory Committee, 30, 64, 71–72, 77, 84, 95–96, 110; financial affairs, 18, 20, 47, 57, 69–71, 79–80, 82–83, 98–101, 107, 109–11, 115–16, 128–31, 136–37; fire at, 58–63, 69, 77; logo of, 35, 47, 61; revolving funds, 18, 20, 25–26, 33, 42. *See also* pressmark
Texas A&M University System, 82, 97, 127; Matching Funds Program, 127
Texas Christian University, 56
Texas Christian University Press, 70, 104
Texas Commerce Bank, 98
Texas Forest Service. *See* Texas A&M University
Texas Historical Commission, 104, 107, 110
Texas Institute of Learning, 102
Texas Institute of Letters, 107, 110
Texas Life Series. *See* Clayton Wheat Williams Texas Life Series
Texas Review Press, 131
Texas-Santa Fe Expedition, 135
Texas Senate, 114
Texas Society of Architects, 107
Texas Southern University, 86
Texas State Historical Association, 70, 100, 102, 104, 107, 110, 134
Texas State Technical College, 98
Texas Tech University Press, 51
Thomas, Alvin A., 54
Thompson, Barry, 97, 118, 127
Thompson, Jerry D., 134
Thompson, Yloundas, 137
Thomson-Shore, Inc., 93
Thornton, Jackie, 137
Toole, John Kennedy, 48
Trinkhaus, Eric, 128
Trogdon, William, 54
Tse-Tung, Mao, 49
Tyler, Ron, 88

Ukraine, 125
University of Alberta Press, 51
University of Arizona Press, 51, 127
University of California-Berkeley, 49, 108
University of California-Los Angeles, 45
University of California Press, 48–50, 52, 54, 88
University of Chicago Press, 71
University of Houston, 115
University of Illinois Press, 33, 35
University of Iowa Press, 51

University of Massachusetts Press, 51
University of Michigan, 128
University of Mississippi Press, 51
University of Missouri, 95
University of Nevada Press, 51, 108
University of New England Press, 51
University of New Mexico, 26, 128
University of North Texas Press, 70
University of Oklahoma, 22, 35
University of Oklahoma Press, 35, 94
University of Pennsylvania Press, 121–22
University of South Carolina, 4, 5,
University of South Carolina Press, 6
University of Southwestern Louisiana, 24
University of Tennessee Press, 94
University of Texas, 4, 7, 8, 11, 73, 78, 101, 128–29
University of Texas at El Paso, 95
University of Texas Press, 7, 8, 11, 19, 26, 32, 39, 69
University of Toronto, 8
University of Utah, 128
University of Virginia Press, 51
University of Washington, 128
University of Washington Press, 38
University of Wisconsin, 73
Uselton, Gene C., 96

Vagabond Hotel, 11
Valdez, David, 132, 134
Vance, Diana Lee, 113, 137
Van Cleef, June, 104–105
Vandiver, Frank E., 28, 30–31, 47, 55, 66, 70, 81, 84, 89, 103, 107, 110, 132–33, 139
van Doorninck, Frederick H., Jr., 74, 76
Vick, Frances Brannen, 127
Vietnam, 42, 108, 126, 133
Verdun, 42

Waco, Tex., 98
Wakefield, Edith, 137
Walker, Robert L., 21, 39, 41, 102
Wallace, Ernest, 101
Walt Disney World Company, 132
Wardlaw, Frank, 3–55, 69, 71, 77, 81, 84–89, 93–94, 99, 104, 106, 110, 122, 132, 135, 138
Wardlaw, Rosemary, 8, 11–14, 36. *See also* Boynton, Rosemary Leonard
Wardlaw Art Collection, 85–88. *See also* Frank H. Wardlaw Collection of Texas Art
Washington, D.C., 15
Washington University, 128
Waters, Michael R., 128
Watriss, Wendy, 105
Watson, Patty Jo, 129
Waur, Roland H., 136
Webb, Walter Prescott, 6, 7, 97
Weems, John Edward, 87
Weirus, Richrd O. ("Buck"), 17, 20, 39, 53
Wells, Clyde H., 10, 63–64
Wesleyan University Press, 17
West, E. Gordon, 87
West, Philip T., 37
West Texas A&M University, 127
West Texas Historical Association, 101
Whelan, Charlotte, 30
Williams, Clayton W., 101, 107
Williams, Clayton ("Claytie") W. Williams, Jr., 101–102
Williams, David Reichard, 106
Williams, Edward B., 126
Williams, Jack K., 3, 5, 10–13, 18, 22, 32, 36, 49, 53, 56–58, 63, 69, 74, 77, 85, 93, 102, 110
Williamson, Jane, 7
Wilson, Woodrow, 124
Winedale Publishing, 131
Winkler, Henry, 5
Winniford, Lee, 133
W. L. Moody, Jr., Natural History Series, 43, 104, 112–13
women, 106, 113
Woodcock, David, 96
Wooster, Robert, 102
World War I, 42, 127
World War II, 23, 41, 49, 91, 98, 101, 103, 104
Wright, William, 104

Yale University, 15, 88, 139

Zeh, Frederick, 126